# THE WAY OF LIVING FAITH

## A Spirituality of Liberation

SEGUNDO GALILEA

*Translated from the Spanish*
*by John W. Diercksmeier*

1817

Harper & Row, Publishers, San Francisco

Cambridge, Hagerstown, New York, Philadelphia, Washington
London, Mexico City, São Paulo, Singapore, Sydney

FIRST EDITION

**Library of Congress Cataloging-in-Publication Data**

Galilea, Segundo.
  The way of living faith.

  Translation of: El camino de la espiritualidad.
  Bibliography: p.
  1. Spirituality—Catholic Church.  2. Catholic Church—Doctrines.  I. Title.
BX2350.65.G3513  1988    248    85–45352
ISBN 0–06–063082–5

88  89  90  91  92  HC  10  9  8  7  6  5  4  3  2  1

# Contents

# Foreword

By Henri J. M. Nouwen

It is a great joy for me to introduce Segundo Galilea's spirituality to North American readers. I still have vivid memories of the day I first met Segundo Galilea. His great vitality, sharp intelligence, deep faith, and burning desire to work for the spiritual renewal of the Church made a deep impression on me.

Shortly after our first conversation he showed me the Spanish text of this book. When I began reading it, I realized that in this text Segundo had summarized his vision of a truly contemporary spirituality, a vision that had grown in depth and breadth during the many conferences and retreats he had given in both North and South America. His vision integrates the new experience of Latin American Christians into the long and rich spiritual tradition of the Church. The struggle for the liberation of the oppressed, the preferential option for the poor, the life of the base communities—all of these new aspects of being Church today have become part of this vital and contemporary spirituality of liberation. Segundo Galilea has not simply written a book to help Latin American Christians with their spiritual life. He has developed a Christian spirituality that gladly receives the new insight and "passion" of the people of God learned in their long, hard journey toward freedom.

As I came to know Segundo better, both as a friend and a spiritual writer, I realized increasingly how much he had to offer North Americans, and my hope grew that his spirituality of liberation would become available in the English language. My Hispanic friend Joseph Nuñez, who initially read the Spanish text of this book, affirmed my conviction that Segundo Galilea's vision reaches far beyond the borders of the Spanish- and Portuguese-speaking world.

I am very pleased that now, several years after my first meeting with Segundo, this important work can also be read by the English-speaking people of the Americas. My own experiences in the Americas have convinced me that a spirituality of liberation is as vital for the North as for the South. Living among the poor of Bolivia, Peru, and Guatemala, I heard an urgent cry for liberation from the forces that keep them in a state of socioeconomic slavery. But living, as I have also done, among the wealthy in North American universities, I felt at least as great an urgency for liberation from the dark forces of guilt, shame, ambition, and depression. Seeing the smiling faces of poor and often undernourished Indian people, and the sad, serious faces of theology students in New England, I was never quite sure who most needed a spirituality of liberation!

In its scope and perspective, Segundo Galilea's book embraces the whole of the Americas. I believe that his work will help to foster important dialogue between the North and the South. Precisely because this book offers not a *theology* but a *spirituality* of liberation, it can fulfill this function. A spirituality directs itself primarily to the question of how to live our daily lives as Christians. Although based on a solid understanding of the teachings of Jesus and his Church, this book focuses upon the implications of those teachings for a life of prayer and service in the name of Jesus. This focus creates a space in which Christians with very different histories can come together and help each other on the way to complete inner and outer freedom.

I would like to bring to the foreground two aspects of Segundo Galilea's book that lead me to view it as an important contribution to the dialogue between North and South American Christians.

First, his vision is centered upon Jesus. Again and again Jesus is presented as the true source for a lived spirituality. This prevents the book from becoming an ideological or merely intellectual treatise, in which such contemporary problems as oppression and poverty, and such contemporary issues as conversion, evangelization, and mission are analyzed or discussed. By keeping his attention upon Jesus, the man of Nazareth in whom God reveals his love for humanity, Segundo moves beyond opinions and arguments. He shows convincingly that we should never turn our gaze away from Jesus. When Jesus remains at the center we will find the strength to create and nourish true community in which we can always find room to confess and forgive.

Second, Segundo never allows us to think of contemplation and action as separate aspects of the Christian life that need to be unified. For him, contemplation is a quality of action and action a quality of contemplation. His Jesus-centered spirituality calls for an intimate, affective bond with the incarnate God as the true source from which every form of authentic action flows. Neither impatient activism nor complacent pietism have a place in this spirituality of liberation. A Christian life, lived in intimate communion with Jesus, is a life in which every moment of the day and night becomes a prayer to God and an act of service to God's people.

I am grateful to Segundo Galilea for writing this book and to John Shopp and John W. Diercksmeier for making it available to the English-speaking world. I pray that it will become an instrument of unity among the Christian communities of North and South America, and thus offer hope, courage, and confidence to many.

# Introduction

## The Current Problem

Christian spirituality has suffered a widespread crisis, not only because it seems to have disappeared or because in many respects its expressions have changed, but above all because its meaning and practice are no longer easily accepted givens. In past centuries, for example, Christians practiced prayer naturally and without asking too many questions. In the past few decades, however, many have called all of this into question. Others have rejected their traditional training and have wanted to substitute in its place (often without success) totally new practices. The word *spirituality* itself has even come under suspicion.

The Christian reaction to this is not wholly unexpected. There is increased discussion today about spirituality, even in the more active and visible sectors of Christianity. Yet, the context is different from what it was; recent generations have experienced profound cultural and religious changes due to the secularization of society and the urgency of social and ministerial tasks. The religious and symbolic sensitivity to the past is not the same as before, nor is the Christian scale of values. Christian commitment has come to hold more importance than the celebration of faith. It is in this new context that the current question concerning the nature of Christian spirituality is being discussed.

Every authentic response to this question must recognize two necessities: the need for a renewal of spirituality to continue in the great spiritual tradition of Christianity, and the need for spirituality to correspond to contemporary human and Christian experiences. For spirituality is nothing more than profound motivations, the mysticism of all human tasks.

Christian spirituality, by its incarnate nature, is not a discipline imposed upon theology, evangelization, or social or family tasks; it is their very source and motivation. When Christians forget or overlook this, they run the risk of a type of schizophrenia. Theology and ethics may be renewed—that is, the view of the relationship between faith and society as well as the function and mission of the Church may change—but if, at the same time, there is not a similar renewal of spirituality, which is the root of these concerns, the spirituality of the past can no longer motivate, and so becomes irrelevant. Spirituality is then perceived as something useless, and is abandoned.

Thus the need to plant the seeds of a renewal of Christian spirituality and faith is an urgent one. This renewal must recover and restore to its rightful place the practice of faith, or religious practice. Because of its very nature, Christian faith must be explicitly practiced or it will die out. Faith and spirituality grow in the measure to which they are exercised by religious means. Faith is a gift from God, specific and irreducible, as fragile as a flower in the desert that needs to be watered and cultivated. This cultivation is even more important in a society and culture that tend to speak less and less about faith. Constant encouragement of the explicit practices of Christian experience is needed.

## Spirituality and Spiritualities

We will avoid a precise definition of spirituality. Defining spirituality is almost impossible, just as defining the life of faith, the Christian life, or even Christianity itself—all of which, in a certain sense, are equivalent terms—is not easy. The root of the difficulty lies in the richness of the Christian idea of spirituality, which causes any definition to remain poor and lacking. Typically, the same thing happens with the majority of basic Christian terms: it is not easy to define evangelization or Church. As in the case of spirituality, these terms can be described and identified as precisely as possible; yet the fact that they often acquire various definitions that are all valid shows that in and of itself, each definition is only partial.

If we were to study what the great Christian spiritual writers understood by spirituality, we would find a number of differing definitions, all of which would be accurate yet nonexclusive. The difference would arise from the spiritual experiences of the authors themselves, from their theology, and so on. Formulations of Christian spirituality, such as "identification with the will of the Father," or "life led by the Spirit," or "imitation or following of Jesus Christ," or "the life of grace," have been and still are normative. Without trying to define the question, we feel that the emphasis that is employed at a certain time or place to determine what spirituality is must be coherent, or in line, with the theological and pastoral emphases of the time and place. For example, the churches of Latin America currently tend to highlight spirituality in its reference to the person of Jesus Christ, to following him and his paschal life. This perspective is appropriate because it is very rooted in the New Testament and includes, at least implicitly, the fundamental elements of Christian spirituality, as well as being culturally significant for Christian communities in that continent.

We can identify Christian spirituality (not only for the Americas but for any place, culture, or social condition) as the process of following Christ, under the direction of the Spirit, and beneath the guidance of the Church. This process is paschal: it gradually leads to identification with Jesus Christ, which in the life of the Christian takes the form of death to sin and selfishness to live for God and for others. To follow and identify with Jesus Christ is to share in his resurrection, stepping with him from death to life, often illustrated by the symbolism of baptism, the objective moment of initiation to spirituality within the personal life of the individual Christian.

Christian spirituality is characterized by its baptismal origin. In baptism, according to St. Paul, "we went into the tomb with Christ and joined him in death, so that as Christ was raised from the dead by the Father's glory, we too might live a new life" (Rom. 6:4). Thus, Christianity is a paschal dialectic of gradual deaths and resurrections in Christ that continually identifies us with him. All of the events of our personal history and of the entire history of humanity are nothing more than the ongoing invitation to this paschal event, which calls each individual and society to be integrated into the mystery of the risen Christ, imitating him in our historical condition.

With this perspective, history and its events are a call to set aside selfishness and be clothed in Christ in order to live for others. And this is still true today in view of current events and challenges. We must follow Jesus of Nazareth, in his paschal reality, into these present-day circumstances. Christian spirituality is historical because in every time and place it supports (and highlights) certain gospel values that in turn inspire the appropriate paths for following Jesus. Yet, at the same time, it is not always the same scale of values that nurture the faith of Christians in the diverse historical experiences of the Church, helping them follow and identify with the crucified and risen Christ.

In this sense, and within a specific Christian spirituality, there may be various "Christian spiritualities." Throughout history, different ages, places, cultures, experiences, and challenges have evoked different spiritualities. These diverse spiritualities do not differ from one another in essence. They possess the same core identity and sources; they always deal with following Jesus. But they differ in the historical and concrete way of following him and, as such, in the values of his message that are emphasized in differing situations, in response to differing challenges, and particularly, in differing cultures.

Let us look at some examples. Christians find themselves in diverse situations and commitments: a contemplative religious, a mother of a family, a missionary. All must follow Jesus according to the Gospel, but because of the form of each life and its challenges, each depends on differing themes and values and responds to certain demands more than others. There are values and demands specific to Christian contemplation, to the Christian family, and to missionary activity. Thus one can rightfully speak of a contemplative or family or missionary spirituality.

Similarly, every historical age shapes and synthesizes (in a different way) its experience of holiness and following Jesus as a result of the prevailing theological ideas and diverse mentalities and cultures of the time. Thus we speak of medieval spirituality, modern devotion, and the like. Christian tasks and experiences also differ, so that each church favors certain Christian demands over others. For example, in the countries of the North Atlantic, there is currently a need to evangelize a technological and secularized world, a need to witness faith in that world, giving rise to a particular spirituality in those Christian areas. In Latin America, on the other hand, the urgency is to evangelize out of social injustices and the reality of the poor and oppressed, leading to a greater reliance on other values and Christian experiences.

The cultural context of faith is another very important factor to consider. Living faith and following Jesus in the midst of rural Brazil are quite different from living the life of faith in the Christian communities of Japan, or among the indigenous peoples of the Andes, or among the Western middle class. These serious differences of mentality and cultural experience give rise to different ways of understanding and achieving spirituality. As a result, we are able to speak of a workers' spirituality, a spirituality of the middle classes, and an Andean or Japanese spirituality.

It also happens that in the life of the Church, not every spiritual experience reaches the point of being recognized by history or theology as spirituality. This may be due to an ecclesial tradition that has not been as attentive to local cultural experiences as it has to certain saints who in their lives achieved the gospel values of their day and who knew how to communicate the experience of their personal spirituality to others. The great currents of spirituality are identified, above all, by their witnesses, saints, or founders, who made explicit in their lives the traces of a particular spiritual experience. In fact, the most well-known spiritualities are those that have some relationship to the spirituality of a saint, such as Franciscan,

Dominican, Ignatian, Carmelite (St. Teresa and St. John of
the Cross), or Benedictine spiritualities. This is quite normal and unavoidable in that for a spirituality to be propagated and recognized as such, it must have the guarantee
of the Church and it must have the means to be communicated, which are conditions met by the spiritualities
of the founding saints. But while honoring the indispensable spiritual experience of the saints, we should pay
more attention to other forms of Christian spirituality
that have no saints or school but that are nevertheless
powerful, such as family spirituality and the spirituality
of liberation.

So, in summary, to understand the various spiritualities throughout history we must keep in mind all of the
factors that have influenced them, including historical,
social, and cultural factors as well as the writings and recognized spiritualities of the saints and founders. These factors have been reflected in various models of the Church.
Let us dwell briefly here on how different models of the
Church, different cultures, different social structures, and
different historical settings affect the various experiences
of Christian faith and spirituality.

### *Spirituality and Models of the Church*

A particular spirituality in history is just one valid way
of living out Christian faith, but it is not an isolated and
autonomous phenomenon. Rather, it is always coherent
with, and the result of, other factors that constitute the
life of the Church in a particular place and time. The
collection of factors that characterize the Church in any
particular place and time is called a model of the Church.
Ordinarily, a certain model of the Church corresponds to

a certain model of pastoral activity, theology, and spirituality, which is exactly what interests us here.

That the institution of the Church and its mission have resulted in differing concrete expressions in history is without a doubt quite obvious. Examples abound. The celebration of the Eucharist in the household communities of the primitive Church is a liturgical model quite different from the celebration of the same Eucharist in the medieval cathedrals, and both are very distinct from present-day celebrations. The model of catechetical instruction in colonial Latin America is not the same as the current model, just as the way of understanding the relation between Church and society has changed, leading to very different models of social pastoral activity. The present model of the bishop is not the same as in the Renaissance Church. The model of mission that the evangelizers brought to the Americas is not the same as that of the current missions in Africa.

In view of the statement that throughout the course of history the Church and its spirituality have been changing—not their identity but rather their models, something that is healthy and unavoidable given the incarnate and visible nature of the Church and Christian spirituality—we can make certain assertions to help us better understand the present crisis in the Church.

*It does not seem fair to judge past models of spirituality from the perspective of our present model of the Church.* Every model must be understood within the context of a particular age, culture, philosophy of life, and missionary challenge for the Church. What makes a model "good" or "bad" is not necessarily its manifestation in history but rather its greater or lesser fidelity to the gospel message, to the Spirit who speaks at a certain time and in a particular social world—that is, its ability to give rise to holiness and mission.

*No model of the Church can claim to be the only or best model, just as one shrub cannot be considered as the only or best possible development of its type of seed.* Always identical with itself, every model is fully the Church; because it is historical, every model is contingent and open to renewal in order to be more authentically the Church. The same holds true for spirituality.

Many think that when changes are introduced into the model of the Church and spirituality that they have always known—something that has happened often in the past few decades—"they are changing the Church." If among simple people this attitude is the result of misinformation or a lack of education, among educated Christians it is known as integralism. The integralist (radical conservative) confuses the theology of the Church with a theological model, the Church with contingent historical models, or Christian spirituality with the way of living faith proper to a particular day and age.

*In the Church, the profound changes that bring new models take place not through rupture but through synthesis.* The idea of rupture in the reform of the Church implies a cutting of ties with the sources, with the life of Christ, which is the life of the Church. Change by rupture is to create another spirituality without continuity with what came before—and therefore without identity or authenticity. In contrast, the idea of synthesis is more appropriate for describing what happens in a renewal of the Church: change by synthesis always conserves what is valid in previous models while renewing it within a new context. Thus spirituality has passed through very diverse historical models—our is not the model of the Middle

Ages—while preserving the true richness of the previous tradition and renewing its ongoing values.

*Renewal by synthesis requires a sometimes very difficult discernment, which has always been a source of argument and controversy, especially during times of transition.* However, if synthesizing—the manner in which the Church changes—offers the guarantee of unity, if it creates consensus and educates faith within a new context, it leads also to the fact that transitions may take a very long time and are always incomplete. Therefore, pure historical models do not exist. No spiritual renewal truly reaches the entire Church. Outdated models may endure for centuries while more recent ones may coexist in times of transition.

Obviously, the coexistence of several models is also a source of conflict which cannot be avoided without sacrificing authentic renewal or tradition. We must learn to live together in communion with these diverse mentalities. Recognizing the model of the Church to which one is referring, with which Christians are identifying, may become one of the keys for solving current disagreements and misunderstandings. Different ecclesiastical models may use the same words—*mission, contemplation, liberation, renewal,* and the like—thus leading to wide divergences.

All of this describes the present crisis in the Church. Where there is transition and renewal, there is always crisis in the sense of a process that creates a synthesis of more adequate values than in the previous synthesis. Crisis is thus inherent in the Church; twenty centuries of history confirm this. We Christians must learn to adhere to the Church in its times of crisis as well as in those times of greater stability; we must learn to live its spirituality in its times of decline as well as its times of renewal.

Due to their global scope and coherence, changes in the models of the Church not only affect its institutions and visible activity but also its mentality, model of theology, and, consequently, its model of spirituality. A certain model of the Church naturally gives rise to a model of theology, in terms of the themes, emphases, and even the methodology that theology tends to adopt. And in the same sense, this gives rise to a model of spirituality. Thus, global renewal of the Church—affecting the model itself—renews all of its aspects sooner or later. This internal interrelationship, this coherence of the institutions of Christianity, makes it impossible for us to write a history of theology while neglecting the other aspects of Christian life in a certain age, such as pastoral activity or its predominant ecclesiology; nor can we create a history of spirituality and disregard the model of the relationship between Church and society or culture, or the model of religious or ministerial life.

### *Spirituality and Its Cultural Context*

The current theology of mission insists upon the profound relationship between Christian faith and culture. This relationship comes as much from the vocation of the Gospel to be spread and shaped according to each culture as from the fact that religion is a component that decisively affects every culture.

This deep relationship between faith and culture also means that culture affects the Christian faith. If we describe a culture as the collective conscience of a human group, constituted by the "group of values that animate it and the 'dis-values' that weaken it," as well as "the forms through which [the people] express and shape them-selves, that is, their customs ... the institutions and struc-tures of social interaction," we understand how all of these cultural factors gradually affect the experience of Christian faith (Puebla 389).

To understand the influence of culture upon spiritu-alities, we must be very precise in specifying the way in which a culture affects the faith of the peoples sharing in that faith. We must realize that cultures do not affect, by themselves, faith and its expressions (spirituality) to the point of being able to deprive them of their Christian identity and authenticity. In spite of the deep relationship that has already been pointed out, faith and spirituality are radically autonomous in the face of any particular culture. But culture does influence faith and spirituality in (1) the truths and values that are, or are not, empha-sized; (2) the way of expressing faith (the "total lan-guage"); and (3) the interpretation and symbolism of the Christian experience. Let us explain further.

*Cultures influence spirituality by the themes and val-ues that are, or are not, emphasized.* This seems evident. When the values of a particular culture coincide with the values of spirituality, these spiritual values are reinforced and favored, giving rise to a certain model of spirituality. On the other hand, the dis-values (or lack of values) in a culture can debilitate the corresponding values of spir-ituality. This may take place with doctrine as well as with the practice of spirituality.

Let us cite some examples. Where a culture upholds the value of solidarity, spirituality will make this value its own; a culture that emphasizes the law and the value of authority will reinforce in its spirituality the virtue of obe-dience and the value of systematic practices. A culture whose peoples are accustomed to suffering will better understand the spiritual theme of the cross, and the cultures of the poor better assimilate a God who is the God of the poor as well as upholding the value of poverty. A culture that is in crisis and loses its values will carry with it a crisis of spirituality.

These mutual influences between faith and culture (one must also remember that faith and spirituality promote and purify cultural values) are even greater the more faith is rooted in the culture. This is the case in some European countries and especially in Latin America. Just as one cannot disregard the reality of Christianity in interpreting those cultures, spirituality itself is also greatly affected by those cultures.

*Cultures influence spirituality because they contribute to the expression of faith and spirituality.* This is also very evident. There are cultures with great expressive and artistic wealth, there are naturally contemplative cultures, and there are affective and sentimental cultures whose discourse is more symbolic than rational. Spiritual expression, therefore, will have the same tendencies. The same thing happens with individualistic, pragmatic, or less symbolic cultures. The spiritualities of these peoples will be very different.

*Cultures blend interpretations of the Christian experience.* That is, the Christian message is received according to the characteristics of each culture, bringing various interpretations to the one Christian experience and spirituality. The Eucharist, for example, has a value in all spiritualities and cultures of Christianity, but it is reinterpreted according to each culture, allowing for a pluralism of spiritualities. Among the indigenous peoples of the Andes, given their religious culture stemming from pre-Christian times, the Eucharist emphasizes the spirituality of sacrifice and adoration; among the Catholic workers, the Eucharist more intensely emphasizes the spirituality of fraternity and justice (that is, in a culture where solidarity is predominant); among social militants, the Eucharist manifests the liberation that comes from Christ; among affluent Christians it comes to mean sharing and being in solidarity with the needy.

The cultural model is thus one of the factors that allows for differentiation among spiritualities. If one speaks of the spirituality of the campesinos, or of urban, indigenous, Latin American, African, or North American spirituality, this is due to one fundamental Christian spirituality being rooted and expressed in these different cultural models.

In the configuration of a cultural-spiritual model, finally, it is important not to lose sight of the economic condition or social class of the people. This powerfully influences the cultural model, and it is equally a common bond in many cultures and spiritualities. Thus, the poorer classes have cultural aspects and religious forms in common, no matter which region they inhabit. This is the grounds, for example, of what may be said about Hispanic religiosity in the United States (or better, Hispanic spirituality), whose common elements are cultural, influenced as well by the economic and social situation the people share.

What has been said does not mean that a particular spirituality is simply reducible to its cultural context or that Christian spirituality is a fact of cultural interpretation. What is decisive about a spirituality is always the experience of faith. But everything previously stated can help us also better interpret (from our current perspective) the great currents or schools of spirituality throughout history. For instance, in Benedictine, Franciscan, or Carmelite spirituality, one must always keep in mind that the fundamental value is a certain way of living faith and love, and of following the person of Jesus Christ. What gives rise to these different schools is that the richness of Christ's ministry is so great and unlimited in terms of the human spirit that it becomes necessary to "specialize" in certain values of his life (fraternity, poverty, mission, one's relationship with the Father, and so on), under the umbrella of love. These spiritualities cannot be understood if one forgets the cultural context of the times in which they were born and in which their founders lived. Acknowledging the influence of culture helps to relativize and provide a proper Christian interpretation of these spiritualities and many of their practices and norms.

## Spirituality and Its Historical and Social Context

The historical and social context in which Christians find themselves in a particular age and place is also a factor in their spirituality. This context is a call from God to certain choices, certain values that are lived out in Christian communities faithful to these challenges, creating a certain spirituality.

The historical and social milieu makes present, through various events and situations, values or countervalues that the person of faith must understand and interpret. This is often what is truly meant by "the signs of the times." These signs, for the Christian, are a call to decipher the new values that history reveals, incorporating them into daily life. Doing this will create a way of Christian life appropriate to that particular historical context, leading the individual Christian to be a witness of the crucified and risen Christ *today* in a special way. We therefore speak of spiritualities for diverse times, adapted to such and such a historical situation. Thus, the age of the Crusades created a spirituality "of crusade," the discovery of America brought about a decidedly missionary spirituality, while the nineteenth century, generally hostile to faith, led to a spirituality of adherence to and defense of faith. One may speak, in all cases, of a Christian spirituality adapted to the times.

This adaptation is not opportunism. It is a process inherent in Christian faith, which is developed and incarnated in diverse persons, circumstances, and epochs. It is a process rooted in a Gospel that is able to embrace every culture and every historical event, creating new forms of expressing faith and the paschal unfoldment of Christian life. It is a process that takes place in times of stability, instability, peace, or injustice. And it takes place today in a time of profound social change.

These profound changes in the social and cultural situation are one of the causes of the crisis of faith and spirituality in the lives of many Christians today. To the extent that faith and spirituality have had insufficient formation and have remained very much tied to a traditional cultural context, static and pietistic, change and new social experiences are not easily integrated into the life of faith, and so that life enters into crisis. The spirituality that nurtured that life falls by the wayside. And this is precisely the challenge facing us: to create a *"new" spirituality,* in the sense already explained above, capable of accepting and expressing itself in times of rapid social change. This challenge requires rereading the Gospel itself, recalling its values, and resituating them in a contemporary setting while at the same time discovering new values. Doing that will lead Christians to a *renewed spirituality*, forming a new gospel synthesis of their relationships with God and with others.

# 1. The Identity of Christian Spirituality

## The Search for the God Who Loved Us First

We must now look closely at precisely those characteristics, those elements, that cause a spirituality to be called Christian, that outline its proper identity as well as its differences from other spiritualities and religions. Facing this question, we sense that Christian spirituality cannot be identified by only one factor or element. Its radical and essential components are many, but at the same time they are inseparable and wholly implied in Christian spirituality itself. (We are referring to those elements that are rooted in, and at the same time give rise to, other characteristics and demands.)

The essential universal element of Christian spirituality is that it is trinitarian. Christian spirituality is a personal relationship with God the Father, with Jesus Christ, and with the Holy Spirit. This colors its more radical characteristics.

In the first place, spirituality has to do with God, and it relates us to God. God is the center and the one absolute reference point of Christian experience. This God is a God who loved us first, who because of this love created us, redeemed us, and liberated us from all evil and slavery, and who through this love revealed and still reveals himself to every people and individual. He is a

God who, out of love, wants to communicate his life to us so that we might truly be his children and share his joy for all eternity.

All spirituality springs from this fundamental fact of a God who loved us first. In our personal relationship, God the Father took the initiative: he loved us first. God sought us out. Our own conversion and Christian path, our own search for God in faith is due to the fact that God seeks us, wants to enter into communion with us, desires our growth, and wills that we be more than we are.

If Christian spirituality is, before all else, an initiative by and a gift from God who loved us and seeks us, spirituality is then our recognition and our response, with all that entails, to this love of God that desires to humanize and sanctify us. The path of spirituality is the process, concrete but never finished, by which we identify ourselves with God's plan for creation. Because this plan is essentially the Kingdom of God and its justice (holiness), spirituality is identification with the will of God for bringing this Kingdom to us and to others. For the authors of classical spirituality, the beginning of all this is desire. In the desire to seek God—or better, to let ourselves be found by God—the Kingdom is realized.

But the human condition being what it is, we are powerless before the God who calls us. We are powerless even to desire God, to recognize his call and seek him. "You would not seek me if I had not already found you." God pulls us out of our blindness and weakness, granting us the gift of faith. Faith is the lifeline that allows us to seek and respond to God. Faith is the experience of our relationship with God. Faith is the most original and fundamental experience of Christian spirituality. And we say that faith is an experience because we are using the term *faith* in its widest sense: that which is inseparable from hope and love. The experience of faith is equally that of hope and love, gifts (theological virtues) that God gives us in order for faith to be alive and operative—that is, that it may be a spiritual experience.

## The Experience of Faith

In this reflection, we will not attempt a systematic study of faith but rather will simply remind ourselves of the basic value of the faith experience in spirituality, while at the same time asking ourselves about the place that faith occupies in our lives.

Through the experience of faith we recognize God, his initial love for us, and the path of our response. This faith, an experience through the hope and love that it generates, is the only possible path of Christian spirituality. The path and search for God is the path of faith, and through the experience of faith is the encounter with God. Because of faith, God is encountered in the measure to which he is sought. Furthermore, as we said before, the crisis of faith is also the crisis of spirituality.

For Jesus himself, faith was the decisive value of discipleship. Any reading of the Gospels reveals the repeated demands of the Lord for his followers' faith (Matt. 8:10, 26; 9:2, 22, 29; 15:28, 31; 16:8, 17; 17:20; 21:21; Mark 2:5; 4:40; 5:34; 6:6; 9:23; 10:55; 11:22; 16:14, 16; Luke 5:20; 7:9, 50; 8:25, 48, 50; 12:28; 17:6; 18:8, 42; John 2:11; 3:15, 36; 4:42, 50, 53; 5:24; 6:29, 36, 40, 47; 8:12; 9:35–39; 11:26, 40; 12:44; 14:12, 29; 16:31; 20:29 . . . ).

At the same time, Jesus considered faith to be a rarity: "I tell you solemnly, if your faith were the size of a mustard seed you could say to this mountain, 'Move from here to there,' and it would move; nothing would be impossible for you" (Matt. 17:20); "But when the Son of Man comes, will he find any faith on earth?" (Luke 18:8).

Today, more than in the past, we realize how difficult it is to believe. It is not easy for those who have faith and it is even harder for nonbelievers. The experience of the world today harshly puts faith to the test. Injustice exists in thousands of forms and rampant misery colors the lives of the majority of the human race. Growing violence and inescapable crises surround us. Millions of our brothers and sisters live in subhuman conditions, destined only to be born, survive, and die. In such a world, it is not easy to have faith, to believe in a personal God who directs history with love. We have come to ask ourselves, anxiously, What good is faith in this situation? What difference does it make to have or not to have faith?

On a deep level, we are frightened and disconcerted by the silence of God. Like the psalmist who is put to the test, we would like God to come to our aid more visibly. We would like God to give proof of his existence and power, to intervene spectacularly in history. We are frightened by God's silence.

Nevertheless this apparent silence is the foundation of our faith. Throughout the history of salvation God has always acted in this way, making room for risk and the option of faith. We are called to discover his presence in the heart of our reality, from the Word of Jesus and not from some direct evidence. For the one who accepts God incarnate in history, for the one who accepts a crucified God who in his abandonment and death transforms slavery, misery, and injustice through liberation, everything is brought to light. Because this acceptance is precisely the conviction of faith, each day it suffers the test of the silence of God in a crucified world. In this way we understand what perhaps we never before took seriously:

the faith is a grace, a gift, fragile and always subject to the possibility of being lost.

We must seriously ask ourselves if God truly is, for us personally, a reality and not just an idea; if in the very real circumstances of everyday life we act, make plans, decide, react as if God were really present in our life. In our ministry are we spending time and energy on the means of action and the preparation and organization of the things we do for God while forgetting God himself? Do we seek God in all things—in our work, in our church, in our apostolate, and our vocation? Finally, have we chosen Christ, have we passed through the crucial choice of the believer between the Gospel and the world?

The need to question our faith is made even more obvious by the present needs of evangelization. In the apostolate, the witness of the personal faith of the apostle is more necessary today than ever before. Often this witness is the only unarguable point. Present generations are unmoved by doctrines and words. They believe only in actions. And the witness of faith is an action. This is the crux of the crisis: that it calls present-day faith into question. We can have long discussions about poverty or prayer and probably leave no one convinced. But the fact of a Christian who has freely chosen poverty or prayer cannot be ignored. In many places, *the only way for the light of Christianity to penetrate is via the gospel life of a person of faith.* What new generations are asking of Christians today is that they consciously live their personal faith.

### *The Merciful Face of God*

Through the experience of faith we are able to recognize and enter into communion with the God who loved us first. In the long process of faith we recognize the true God, we purify our image of him, we experience the unique and unmanipulable God, the Christian God, God the Father of Jesus Christ. The knowledge and experience of the true face of God are the primary demand that identifies Christian spirituality.[1]

Let us not think, *a priori,* that a Christian believes in and prays to the Christian God: there are always ambiguities and idolatries in the God who is adored and followed. Knowledge of and conversion to the God of the Gospels is a lifelong task, for everyone. Spirituality is the gradual conversion to the God of Jesus.

Or do we believe that the image of God held by a peasant in the Andes is the same image held by an upper-middle-class Christian? Does a religious community in New York "pray to the same God" as a community in Guatemala? It is true that we are basically speaking of the same Christian God, but it is equally true that this God needs to be "purified" and "evangelized" in these cases. Cultural context, social condition (wealth, poverty, insecurity, well-being), history of the individual or of the people, even the individual or collective temperament, condition and even deform the authentic image of the God of Jesus. Social groups and cultures create idols, and these idols are intermixed with the one true God, obscuring him.

Every spiritual journey, as we see it above all in the saints, is a maturing of the living idea of God. The God of the Christians reveals himself gradually, according to the measure of the fidelity and contemplative growth of the believer ("No one knows the Father except the Son, and those to whom the Son wishes to reveal him" [Luke 10:22]). The biblical God is not the God of theodicy or of pure rationality; he is a God who must be encountered, who must be received as a gift and a revelation. He is a different God.

The Christian God is not the God of the philosophers, of logic, or of theists. Belief in God does not make the Christian. A Christian is someone who has discovered the biblical God, the God of Abraham, Moses, and the prophets, the God who is fully revealed in the God of Jesus. The history of salvation is a progressive and gradual revelation of the face of the one true God. The path of spirituality, today and always, is the leading of individuals and cultures through this gradual revelation, even within different contexts and experiences.

In the experience of Abraham, God is revealed as a historical God who intervenes in the life of persons to commit himself to them and to form a people with them. "Go forth from your land ... to a land that I will show you. I will make of you a great nation, and I will bless you; I will make your name great" (Gen. 12:1ff.). The God of the Bible is the God of commitment, of the covenant, of the promise. "Between you and me I will establish my covenant and I will multiply you exceedingly.... My covenant with you is this: you are to become the father of a host of nations.... I will maintain my covenant with you and your descendants after you throughout the ages as an everlasting pact, to be your God.... On your part you and your descendants after you must keep my covenant..." (Gen. 17:1ff.). He is a God in whom the individual must place hope against all hope, who must be trusted, who must be believed absolutely, to whom one must be faithful. "By faith Abraham obeyed when he was called, and went forth to the place he was to receive as a heritage; he went forth, moreover, not knowing where he was going.... By faith Abraham, when put to the test, offered up Isaac; he who had received the promises was ready to sacrifice his only son" (Heb. 11:8–17).

This absolute God, faithful to his promises but thirsty for the faith and trust of humanity, reveals himself to Moses in a new way. The religious experience of Moses has already carried him to contemplation of the God of his fathers, holy and totally Other, yet a protagonist in the history of his people. "God called out to him from the bush ... 'Come no nearer! Remove the sandals from your feet, for the place where you stand is holy ground. I am the God of your father ..'" (Exod. 3:4ff.).

But perhaps more to his surprise he discovers that his God is also a God of justice, a God concerned about the suffering and oppression of his people, a liberating God. "I have witnessed the affliction of my people in Egypt and have heard their cry of complaint against their slave drivers, so I know well what they are suffering. Therefore I have come down to rescue them from the hands of the Egyptians ..." (Exod. 3:7–8). The Christian God is the liberator of the oppressed. He is the God of hope for the poor.

The experience of the prophets is one of perceiving that this God is always in danger of being replaced by ever newer man-made idols, such as religious and political idols and the idols of human pride and emotion. The prophets, without exception, do nothing else but announce the true God and denounce all of the idolatries that deform him. The prophets are the great purifiers of the idea of God. Their God, the biblical God, is a jealous God, jealous of sin, of every evil and every idolatry. He is a God to whom one must be converted.

In this conversion, the prophets reveal to us another surprising aspect of the face of the God of the Bible: to be converted to him is to be converted to one's neighbor. It is to practice charity, justice, and mercy. "Releasing those bound unjustly, untying the thongs of the yoke; setting free the oppressed and breaking every yoke; sharing your bread with the hungry, sheltering the oppressed and the homeless; clothing the naked when you see them, and not turning your back on your own.... Then you shall call, and the Lord will answer ..." (Isa. 58:6–9).

The last prophet, John the Baptist, reveals to us what the previous prophets have already announced; namely, that one cannot come to the true God, or even comprehend him, without a change of life and heart. The Christian God is a God who must be encountered, and who is encountered in the measure to which he is sought; he is sought in conversion and in the exodus from the idols that replace him in the life of the individual. Conversion to the Christian God and conversion to one's neighbor are one and the same thing (Luke 3:10).

In the person of Jesus Christ, the Christian God is shown to us in his definitive fullness and purity. "The grace of God has appeared, offering salvation to all ..." (Titus 2:11). Jesus recapitulates all of the traces of the biblical God from Abraham to the prophets. Jesus makes God accessible and experiential to all persons; in Jesus, God takes on human qualities. The historical God becomes history; the God of the poor becomes poor; the God of justice becomes the victim of injustice; the God of the promise gives his life to fulfill it; and the God of hope gives us security forever (John 1:18).

In his revelation to us, Jesus reveals the essence of the Christian God: to be pure love and mercy, active, dynamic, and limitless. Because God is love, he is committed to his people. Because he is love, he is faithful to his promises. Because he is love, he is justice and liberation for the poor, hope and refuge for sinners. Because he is love, he is jealous of the idols that deform his love and so deform the individual. Because he is love, he is in solidarity with human history, to the point of his sacrifice on the cross. The cross and Christ's suffering mean that the Christian God loves to the point of suffering (the proof of true love) and that his love is not that of an immutable and distant God. Contrary to the God of reason and theodicy, of paganized or deformed images, the Christian God makes himself vulnerable out of love. He makes himself truly Father of each person. He makes us his children. And he identifies himself with the most disgraceful of us (Matt. 25:40).

To purify through the experience of faith our idea of God is to identify him with this real, historical, and demanding love, to take the consequences of this in spirituality, in pastoral activity, and in the Church, which is the sacrament of the God of love. He is the only measure for appreciating any spirituality, any institution, or any missionary endeavor. He is the heart of the Christian message.

The central question of spirituality in the contemporary world is how the Church of God and all Christians can communicate the true God of Jesus to the world. Only this God is believable, desirable, and able to pierce the wall of idolatry and indifference. This leads us to the ever-present demand that Christians be continually converted to the God of Jesus Christ.

### Following Jesus Christ

If God has revealed himself uniquely and fully in Jesus Christ (Heb. 1:1–3), then there is no way of seeking and finding God but through knowing and following Jesus Christ. For Jesus Christ is known in the measure to which he is followed and imitated (John 14:5–11). Thus following Jesus Christ is the most fundamental and original dimension of Christian spirituality.[2]

The originality and authenticity of Christian spirituality consists in this: that we follow a God who took upon himself our human condition, One who had a history like ours, who lived our experiences, who made choices, who devoted himself to a cause for which he suffered, who had successes, joys, and failures, for which he gave his life. That man, Jesus of Nazareth, like us in everything but sin, and in whom lived the fullness of God, is the only model for our discipleship.

For this reason the starting point of our Christian spirituality is the encounter with the humanity of Jesus. This is what gives Christian spirituality all its realism. In making the historical Jesus the model of our discipleship, Catholic spirituality uproots us from the illusion of "spiritualism," of an "idealistic" Christianity, of values that are abstract and alien to historical experiences and demands. It frees us from the temptation of adapting Jesus to *our* ideals, to *our* interests.

Our spirituality has to recover the historical Christ. This dimension has frequently been played down in our Latin American tradition. This tradition has a tendency to "dehumanize" Jesus Christ, to emphasize his divinity without giving enough emphasis to his humanity, with all its consequences. The Jesus of "power," extraordinary, miraculous, purely divine, hides Jesus as a historical model of discipleship.

It is only through Jesus of Nazareth that we can know God, his words, his deeds, his ideals, and his demands. It is in Jesus that the true God reveals himself: all-powerful but at the same time poor and suffering for love; absolute, but also someone with his own human history, someone close to every person.

Only in the historical Jesus can we truly come to know the values of our own Christian life. There is always the danger of formulating these values from fixed ideas and definitions:

"prayer is this . . . ," "poverty consists in this other . . . ," "fraternal love has these certain characteristics . . ." But just as we don't know who God is unless we discover him through Jesus, we can never really know what prayer is, what poverty is, what fraternity or celibacy is except in the way Jesus came to know these values. Jesus is not only a model of living; he is the root of the values of life.

Thus any real following of Christ springs from a knowledge of his humanity, his personality traits, his way of acting, which by themselves make up the demands of our Christian life.[3]

Jesus not only teaches us how to live as Christians, in communion with God the Father; he also teaches us how to live as human beings. Jesus is not only the sacrament of God; he is also the human ideal. He is the root of authentic humanism. Jesus teaches us to love, to work, to suffer, to surrender ourselves to some purpose, to have hope, and also to die, as true human beings. Christian spirituality is also human spirituality; it is the peak of humanism.

We are speaking now of the *following* of Christ rather than the *imitation* of Christ. Both are legitimate expressions in the Christian tradition, and they have served to synthesize the path of spirituality. But we currently prefer following to imitation because following seems more dynamic, like an unfinished task along the path of life. We are not speaking of a literal imitation of Jesus: we cannot reproduce everything that Jesus lived in his time, nor are we called to copy him in all of the contingencies of his life. We are speaking more of identifying with the attitudes, the spirit, and the values that Jesus incarnated in the circumstances of his time and that today we must incarnate (follow) in the circumstances of our own history.

Christ, known and incarnated in faith and love, is the heart of following him. Christ is followed as long as we deepen our knowledge motivated by faith and desire to be like him, carried along by love. Following him is much more than pursuing christological and biblical studies; it is an encounter in faith and love appropriate to the wisdom of the Spirit and Christian contemplation. If means knowing the Lord who we follow contemplatively, with our entire being, especially the heart, like a disciple and not a student, like a follower and not a detective. Here again we see what is original about Christian spirituality: we do not know Jesus except by following him. The Lord's face is revealed to us in the experience of following him. Therefore, Christology is contemplative, leading to the praxis of the imitation of Jesus.

Now let us not think that this contemplative and imitative knowledge of Jesus is easy. It goes beyond analysis and reason. St. Paul speaks to us of a "hidden wisdom that comes from God" (1 Cor. 1:30; Eph. 1:9), and he also tells us that "he counted everything as loss" (Phil. 3:8) to him in comparison to this knowledge of the Lord (Gal. 1:16). The revelation of Christ in us, the contemplative Christology of which we speak, is a gift of the Father. To receive this as wisdom and not just as knowledge demands of us a great poverty of spirit along with the gifts of the Holy Spirit, who breathes where it will.

We can prepare for this contemplative revelation of Jesus by immersing ourselves in faith in the Gospel and by disposing ourselves as disciples in order to learn what this Word teaches us about the Lord. We can have a solid Christology and exegesis but these can never take the place of the contemplation of the Gospel. The Gospel transmits to us what most deeply impressed the apostles and the first disciples; it was brought together in the tradition of the first communities to recall what was most significant for the faith and spirit of the Christians. "What we have heard with our ears and seen with our eyes, what we have looked upon and touched with our hands concerning the word of life, we proclaim also to you ..." (1 John 1:1).

For this reason the Gospel is irreplaceable. We find in it Christology as wisdom, and the image of Christ as the inspiring message of all discipleship. We find there a person whom we can imitate out of love.[4]

This path of imitation and following is the path of Christian spirituality. We find all of the values, demands, and experiences of this spirituality in the life and practice of Jesus himself. He is the one who grounds and shows the way for our calling to seek God and to live out of his life and intimacy. Jesus was above all the man committed to the Father, who sought the Father's face and will to the point of his sacrifice on the cross; who lived in absolute intimacy with the Father; who constantly expressed this intimacy in his prayer and adoration to the Father, who was for Jesus the inexhaustible source of his human fidelity (Mark 1:35; Luke 4:42; Phil. 2; Luke 22:39–46). It is Jesus' practice that teaches us to relate to others in fraternity and love, to give witness to and fight for truth and justice; that gives meaning to the option for the poor and suffering as well as the love of one's enemy; that teaches us the value of the cross, poverty, and humility; that teaches us how to be faithful in human and Christian commitments. To develop these themes, to see the conditions that following Jesus imposes on Christians today, is Christian spirituality. This has been the task of the past few pages, and will be what concerns us in the chapters to follow.

That all of the great movements of spiritual renewal in the Church have given a central place to the humanity of Jesus and to the imitation and following of this humanity should not surprise us. St. Francis made imitation *sine glossa* of the Jesus of the Gospels as the springboard for his spiritual revolution. For St. John of the Cross, following Christ (a "continual appetite" for imitating and being identified with his spirit) was "the power line" of the entire way of Christian perfection toward union with God. St. Ignatius conceived his Exercises—the key and synthesis of his spiritual renewal—as a meditation on and contemplation of the great moments of Jesus' life, to imitate him in the discernment of our own life. For St. Teresa of Avila, reference to the humanity of Jesus was so fundamental that she made his imitation the only concrete way of verifying degrees of prayer and mystical experiences. Closer to our own time, strong movements of spirituality like those originated by Charles de Foucauld, devotion to the Heart of Jesus, and even the incipient spirituality of liberation, have been based on a rediscovery of following Jesus according to the Gospels.

### The Path of Discipleship

We now see more clearly that the fundamental value of spirituality is that of making us disciples of Jesus—that is, making us Christians. This is the heart of the Gospel and of the spiritual wisdom of the Church. The various schools and specializations of spirituality, the diverse vocations and ministries, serve simply to describe this fundamental value. Any form of spirituality, vocation, or ministry in the Church, no matter how important, cannot substitute for the fundamental call of every human being to follow Jesus, to learn, little by little, to be a Christian.

Today we seem better able to sense that the objective of any spirituality, of any station if life or ministry, is essentially to make us Christians, followers of Jesus in the

Church. No one is yet the Christian that Christ wants him or her to be. To become a Christian is a lifelong process; no ministry or vocation can take this for granted.

When Jesus conferred on Peter his ministry in the Church (John 21:15ff.), he did so because Peter was ready to follow him, by the particular path of the exercise of his ministry. "Peter, do you love me?... Then tend my sheep ... and follow me." Like all disciples of Christ, then as now, Peter was a Christian—but not completely. He had to become one. The fidelity required of him as head of the Church was for him the path to becoming a Christian.

So monks are not Christians who "specialize"; they are those who, through their charismatic vocation, are learning to be Christians. Their religious life is the garden in which they grow as disciples of Christ. In the same way, through their ministry, bishops and priests must be "models of the Christian community" (St. Paul) although this is not a professional title but a witness to aspire to, as long as that ministry leads them to be ever better believers. The best thing that could ever be said about a bishop is that he is a good Christian, an evangelical individual.

Therefore, all believers, whatever their ministry or specific vocation may be, must encounter basically the same challenges on the path of spirituality. Contemplation, commitment, the cross, radical fraternity, freedom, and faith are all conditions for following Christ, as necessary as they are arduous for bishops and lay Christians alike.

## Life According to the Spirit

Christian spirituality is trinitarian. It is not only following the incarnate Son who leads us to the Father. It is also living through the Holy Spirit and being led by the Spirit. This is equally essential to Christian identity.[5]

Christ, sent from the Father, acts today (after his resurrection) through his spirit. The Holy Spirit is the spirit of Christ, who pushes and leads us in following Jesus.

In other words, Christian spirituality is not only following Jesus (Christ as the Way) but at the same time it is living the life of Jesus (Christ as the Life), through the Spirit. Through the spirit (the life) that Christ shed upon the world and particularly upon those who would be his disciples, we not only imitate Christ but we also transform ourselves into Christ and—like him—into children of God. This is what has come to be called the life of grace, becoming new people, being "born again," as Jesus said to Nicodemus (John 3:1–15). This personal and collective rebirth of the believer is the work of the Spirit. It is life according to the Spirit.

The gift of the Spirit is also collective. It was offered at Pentecost to the apostles and to the people who listened to it. The Spirit is offered today to the people, to society, to cultures, and, in a full and decisive way, to the Church. Life in the Church is life in the Spirit; to renew ourselves and to renew the Church is to let ourselves be led by the Spirit.

From its beginnings, Christian tradition has attributed to the Holy Spirit everything that is dynamic in Christianity. The Church has us pray and ask the Spirit to "renew the face of the earth" and to "recreate all things." For the Church, the Spirit is the "giver of life" and the "Spirit of truth" (John 16:13), who in history leads Christians to be renewed continually according to the truth of the gospel. The Spirit guarantees the youth of the Church, its institutions and choices, and its Christian life. Wherever there is renewal according to truth, there is the Spirit: the source of life (John 7:38) of every dynamic and every renewal. This animating force of the Spirit, expressed in different historical and social contexts of Christianity, gives rise to what we call spirituality.

Life according to the Spirit, how Christians live the demands and tasks of their faith in a certain historical and social context, is not independent of the historical, social, and cultural dynamics of the place in which that faith is lived. The Spirit is fully communicated to the Church, but also manifests itself in the dynamics of history and society, in its values, its hopes, its ideals and tasks, inasmuch as they coincide with the values of the Kingdom.

For this reason, Christ is the Lord of history who "gives light to every man coming into the world" (John 1:9). Thus there are two reasons Christ is the Lord of the Church, living in his Church through the Spirit who leads the disciples to follow him and to live his life. For this reason, too, when one speaks of the spiritual life one is referring not simply to a life guided by the individual's superior faculties but rather to a life oriented to and nourished by the spirit of Jesus, as a "new creation" (Rom. 8:11; Titus 3:5).

The risen Jesus not only sent us his spirit. He himself, in his earthly life and activity, fully incarnated that spirit, allowing himself to be totally led by it, to the point of manifesting it in his resurrection (Pentecost): the action of Christ who lives with the Father and the action of the Spirit are the same thing, due to the total fidelity of Jesus of Nazareth to the Spirit who led him (Rom. 8:9–11; 1 Cor. 6:11; 2 Cor. 3:18; 13:13; Gal. 2:17; Eph. 4:30).

Jesus' humanity is our model because he realized radically that to which we are all called: to live according to the Spirit. Jesus is also the model of the spiritual life, of Christian spirituality, because his life and actions were guided and nourished by the Holy Spirit. In Jesus, and in the disciples called to follow him, life according to the Spirit is opposed to "life according to the flesh," "according to the world" (Gal. 5:19–21; John 6:33). To live according to the flesh, as opposed to the Spirit, is not so much to live according to sin and passions but rather, more profoundly, to live in a solely earthly and temporal perspective, closed in on oneself. It is to live by the criteria and "standards of this age" (Rom. 12:2). To live according to the Spirit, however, is to live according to the criteria and perspectives of God, which have been incarnated for all time in the life and teachings of Jesus.

Christian spirituality attributes to the Holy Spirit everything that leads believers to identify with the life of Jesus. Entering the faith, the path of conversion, the knowledge and love of Jesus Christ, and the desire to follow him are due to the intervention of the Spirit. Christian prayer is possible because of the Spirit who lives within us (Rom. 8:26–27). Charisms, ministries, calls, and vocations to the community are always interventions of the Spirit, who leads believers to follow Jesus in specific ways.

The Word of God and the sacraments are, in Christian life, an encounter with the sanctifying and liberating Jesus, through the Holy Spirit who nourishes and gives life to them. The mission of the Church is only successful in spreading the Kingdom because of the Spirit who animates the Church's activity and nourishes its preaching and works.

In a very profound way, life according to the Spirit makes available to us the norms, wisdom, and spiritual sensitivity with which Jesus lived and acted. Life according to the Spirit sends us the "mentality" and the "customs" of God. The actions and gifts of the Holy Spirit in the disciples refer to this. Sharing in the mentality and the customs of Jesus infused by the Holy Spirit enables us to discern and act evangelically. A good part of spirituality consists in discerning and carrying out the realizations and paths with which God calls us and makes himself present in our lives.

Finally, the universal activity of the Holy Spirit in humans means that even those who lack faith and who do not consciously follow Jesus Christ are able to share in the redemption and grace of the Kingdom. As long as these individuals are faithful to the activity of the Spirit in their lives, they participate in some way in the norms and practice of Jesus, which we might call the spirit of Jesus. Thus these individuals have an unconscious experience of the dynamics of Christian spirituality. Those who have this experience outside of the Church have it due to a gift of the Holy Spirit.

When the Holy Spirit acts in nonbelievers, or in historical events, it acts as the spirit of Jesus Christ; it inspires attitudes and actions that conform to the law of Christ and his Kingdom, even though the protagonists do not know it. There is always continuity between what the Spirit does and the imitation of Jesus. Thus those who do not have the Christ of the Gospels as a conscious norm of life but who do accept the dynamics of the Holy Spirit within them share the spirit of Jesus or the spirit of the Gospel in their fruits of justice and love.

On the other hand, because of a lack of fidelity to the Spirit, there are believers who accept Christ as God and as master of life but who do not conform to his demand of following him. These individuals believe in Christ, but insufficiently; they do not follow the spirit of Christ that is essential to Christian life.

Christian spirituality in its fullness is the synthesis between the spirit of Jesus and the acceptance of his person and Gospel. Those who believe in Jesus need help to live according to his practices—that is, to acquire the spirit of Jesus. Orthodoxy without practice and appropriate attitudes is insufficient and incoherent.

In the same way, living the spirit of Jesus in various aspects of life is insufficient without an explicit reference to Jesus and his Gospel, because in this case there is no Christian coherence. The Holy Spirit acts outside of the Church in some lives and events (giving rise to the values of the Kingdom here and there), but what gives integrity to these events is following Christ. Christ makes fidelity to the Spirit something global, coherent, and permanent. Living the Christian spirit without Jesus is always precarious and incomplete. It is always subjective, in danger of being an ideological spirituality, partial and eventually contradictory. In contrast, Christian spirituality must be integrally liberating and humanizing. The key to this spirit and this integral ethic is the humanity of Jesus recognized and followed in the Church. This, in a definitive way, is what the Spirit leads us toward.

### *The Guidance of the Church and the Community*

The guidance of the Church, mother and teacher of the Christian life and the experience of the Church, is also an essential component of spirituality. The Church is the homeland, the privileged place where the Holy Spirit exists and acts. The Church is the sacrament of Christ and of following him; it is the most authentic and primordial place for the encounter with the Father.

The Church is not an arbitrary mediation that interposes itself between ourselves and the Holy Spirit. On the contrary, it is the guarantee that the spirit of Christ is among us and that we can follow him without being tricked. The Church is not the Holy Spirit, but it incarnates and discerns it. The Church is not Jesus Christ, but through its word and teachings of faith and through its sacraments and pastoral service it leads us toward participation in the life of Christ.

This is not the place to develop an entire ecclesiology but rather to reflect on Christian spirituality and the role of the Church. A temptation has always existed toward a spirituality and a Christianity without recourse to the Church, to its spiritual tradition, and to what it offers us as the experience of God. But the truth is that there is no true spirituality without the Church. Christian spirituality is neither an ideology nor a mere ethical attitude that can be fed from any source. Christian faith and its spirituality, as life according to the Spirit, have a source of nourishment and experience that the Holy Spirit has united indissolubly and efficaciously. This source is the Church.

The Church is the fount of, and offers us the indispensable sources of, Christian spirituality. We will return to this in the following chapter.

A spirituality that does not share in the life of the Church, its sacraments, its communities and movements, its preaching and formation of faith, and so on, ends by being extinguished or by becoming sectarian and subjective. By participating in the Church, we not only proclaim belief in life according to the Spirit but we also gain the concrete criteria for living by the Spirit and following Jesus in our individual circumstances.

The role of the Church as guide for spirituality is to assure that our life according to the Spirit is not merely subjective but rather that it is objectively in accord with the Gospel and the practice of Jesus. The Church as guide, with all its forms of service to the faith, helps us objectively to recover, here and now, the paths of the Gospel in our individual history.

Along the same lines, the Church is the guide for spirituality because it introduces and leads us to a sharing in the great spiritual tradition of Christianity. Any renewal, any creation, any historical realization of Christian spirituality is unsound and inauthentic if it does not embrace and if it does not relive the values and fundamental experiences of the Christian mystical tradition. In other words, even in other contexts, no "new" spirituality can allow itself to ignore the teaching and secular experience of the Church, which it uses today to guide us along the path of the Spirit.

This is where the great spiritual masters of the Church acquire a primordial value: the Church offers their thought to us today as a guide. We can mention, of course, the New Testament, the Fathers of the Church, and the great mystics. With their support, the Church guides us today along the arduous and often dark path of spirituality. Everything valid that we find among the modern books on spirituality is nothing but the present-day actualization of this great tradition.

Following from this, we must emphasize the role of the Christian community. The community of the Church in which a Christian ordinarily and in fact participates— the Christian base community, the apostolic team, the parish, the religious community, or the like—is the very concrete and local way through which the Church acts as spiritual guide. The directions of the Church and of the spirituality giants are not sufficient by themselves to guide many Christians who do not have access to them or who, in any event, must make discernments about very concrete problems and situations.

In the communal celebration of faith, in the interchange and study of the Word of God, in the common search for Christian commitment, and in the renewal of life, the ecclesial community guides its members, in reciprocal assistance, to be living Christians.

Christian spirituality requires the backing of the community; it is communitarian. It is communitarian because the diverse ecclesial communities—commensurate with the differing degrees of their participation—are the place and event for the experience of Church. The Church as the place for life according to the Spirit and as locus of encountering and following Jesus becomes the vital experience in the life of the community. The community channels the basic sources of spirituality to believers: the presence of the spirit of Christ among them ("Where two or three are gathered in my name, I will be there among them" [Matt. 18:19]), the word and sacramentality of the Church, and the experience of fraternal love. The community is a spiritual experience because it is the experience of fraternity, love, and solidarity.

### *The Revisioning of Life*

The Christian community is also a spiritual guide because it helps us discern the demands of the Spirit in our daily life. While the spiritual tradition of the Church guides us in the larger matters of the Spirit, such as how and under what conditions and how often to pray and receive the sacraments, how to read the Bible, how to live in love and fraternity, what it means today to do justice, and how to overcome our blindness and sin, guidance in how to apply these teachings to our daily life comes from our concrete Church community. Such application and discernment are necessary if we are to revision our lives.

In revisioning our life, we view the facts and situations of our life, in which we must discern what attitude to take and what to do as Christians, within the context of the community, the Church. We also view the aspirations, callings, and inspirations that we believe come from the Spirit. Interchange with the community brings to these life events—which are collectively experienced by others— the light and discernment that come from the word of the Gospel and the thinking of the Church. This process of mutual illumination and fraternal assistance helps us slowly and gradually to discern what is true and false in our norms, attitudes, and responses to the Spirit. This process gives us true spiritual guidance, not by immediately solving all problems or by judging the lives of others, but by allowing us to question in an atmosphere of faith and fraternity, where it becomes easier for Christians to encounter the true path of the Spirit.

The revisioning of life is often systematic, achieved by way of a certain method, as in many lay movements. However, more often it is spontaneous; it takes place in communities, among other Christians, without conscious reflection upon revisioning one's life. It is in this way that many communities manifest their fidelity to the Gospel.

Many times, however, the revisioning of life in community is not enough to enable one to discern and be guided along the paths of the Spirit. There are times when a person has delicate problems and experiences whose interpretation requires counsel from someone with a greater knowledge of the person and his or her Christian history, or with greater wisdom and spiritual knowledge. These are times when what the Christian needs is not so much a revisioning in community as a revisioning with the aid of another person capable of proper discernment. This is called spiritual direction. Spiritual direction, understood as life renewal with the aid of another person, whatever shape it has taken throughout history, whatever its relative importance with respect to the ecclesial community, is also one of the significant ways in which the Church guides us. It is the representation of the ecclesial community in a brother or sister who helps and guides us to live according to the Spirit.

## An Incarnate Spirituality

The incarnation of faith, hope, and love that comes to us from the spirit of Christ is an essential and original aspect of Christian identity. The search for God, following Jesus, and living in the Spirit must become part of our personal and collective history.

Spirituality is incarnated within the context of Christian life, just as the Son of God was incarnated within the context of human condition. Christian life has many global dimensions, and is like human history, in which people, events, and even nature itself are the means by which God acts, speaks to us, and reveals himself. The Christian experience of God takes place within human experiences.

In this sense, Christian spirituality in its fullness can be considered as a type of humanism. There is no Christian demand or experience that is not humanizing, and the paths of the Spirit would not be authentic if they did not also lead to human liberation. In another way, Christian spirituality supersedes merely temporal human–centered perspectives, uncovering the demands, purifications, and liberations that make the human person greater, opening humanism to the following of Jesus Christ.

The incarnate condition of spirituality, making life according to the Spirit into a transcendent humanism, is what undergirds the apparent paradoxes of Christian mysticism. Incarnate spirituality is centered in the search for God through Jesus, but it is also centered on the individual and the search for fraternal love. It lives in the hope for the Kingdom without end, but it is completely involved in the tasks of the Kingdom within history and society. It receives faith as a gift from God, irreducible to any human experience, but it knows that this faith takes on human flesh and demands according to diverse cultures, the challenges of society, and individual commitments. It knows that the experience of God is inseparable from commitment, and that every human or Christian commitment must also be the place for the experience of God.

To pursue this theme would be repetitious. We have already detailed various aspects of the incarnation of spirituality. Later we will elaborate on the incarnation of spirituality in the psychological makeup of individuals, in human love, and in mission, especially among our neighbors and the poor. The privileged "place" in which spirituality is incarnated and becomes practice is in love toward our brothers and sisters and in preferential love for the poor and suffering. All of the incarnations of mysticism, all of the realism of the Christian spirit, and all of the demands of the practice of faith and love find expression in love for our brothers and sisters, the poor. Finding God hidden in the faces of our brothers and sisters is the ultimate experience of the incarnation of Christian spirituality.

## REFERENCES

1. Leonardo Boff, *La Experiencia de Dios* (Bogotá: CLAR, 1975); C. Ducoq, *Dios Diferente* (Salamanca: Sigueme, 1978); J. Danielou, *Dios y Nosotros* (Madrid: Taurus, 1966).
2. C. Ducoq, *Jesus Hombre Libre* (Salamanca: Sigueme, 1978); John Sobrino, *Christology at the Crossroads* (Maryknoll, N.Y.: Orbis Books, 1978); José Comblín, *Jesus of Nazareth* (Maryknoll, N.Y.: Orbis Books, 1976); Segundo Galilea, *Following Jesus* (Maryknoll, N.Y.: Orbis Books, 1981); Charles de Foucauld, *Spiritual Writings;* St. Ignatius of Loyola, *The Spiritual Exercises* (Chicago: Loyola University Press, 1951), especially the Second and Third Weeks.
3. Segundo Galilea, *Following Jesus* (Maryknoll, N.Y.: Orbis Books, 1981), 12–13.
4. Ibid., 14.
5. CLAR, *La Vida según el Espíritu en las Comunidades Religiosas de América Latina* (Bogotá: CLAR, 1973).

# 2. The Sources of Spirituality

## The Word of God and the Gospel

The Word of God is the primordial source for Christian spirituality because it gives rise to faith. The experience of faith is the core of spirituality, just as the Word is the root of faith. All other sources of spirituality—the sacraments and the like—presuppose and celebrate a faith that had its origin in the faithful hearing of the Word.

This is a fact of the Christian experience, and a witness to the Bible. For St. Paul, faith comes from the preaching of the Word (Rom. 10:14). For Jesus, the authentic follower is the one who hears the Word, keeps it, and puts it into practice (Matt. 7:21ff.; Luke 11:27–28), where the spiritual reward is in proportion to the acceptance of the Word.

Experience tells us that what most sustains us and strengthens our faith is listening adequately to the Word of God in any of the varied ways in which the Church offers it to us, such as the proclamation of the Bible in the community, preaching, exhortations, retreats and study sessions, catechesis, liturgy, and the like.

We see again that the Church is of necessity the context that gives rise to our faith and that the Word of God is the spoken word in the Church, in the Christian community. The Bible itself, the Word of God through antonomasia, is written as the experience of the Church, the people of God, and the first communities.

In the same way we can appreciate the enormous importance of personal contact with the Word of God, of private reading of the Bible and the great spiritual authors or books on spirituality. What has traditionally been called spiritual reading, on many accounts a more personal and private listening to the Word, is a very important and recommended practice for maintaining one's life of faith. It becomes even more important when Christians have little opportunity for hearing the Word of God in community or publicly proclaimed. Just as everyone who reads has bedside books, so should the Christian, and among them should be the Bible—especially the New Testament and above all the Gospels—and one or more Christian books that have been or are of help. Many people run the risk of extinguishing their faith by not listening to or reading the spoken or written words of God in the Church.

We must stress the fact that the Bible remains the source and paradigm of every Word of God. The Church is inspired and sets its norms by it, in all of the varied forms of announcing the Word of God. The Bible is the Word of God in its truest and most literal sense; listening to it and having periodic contact with it can generate faith in a way unparalleled by any other aspect of Christian spirituality.

In the Christian reading of the Bible, the Gospels occupy the central place. The Gospels are the Word of God in the most real sense because the words and attitudes of God himself are recorded there. We have already pointed out that the necessary access to the humanity of God, to knowing and following him through love, is through the Gospels. In the extreme case, a Christian may be able to ignore the other books of the Bible, but not the Gospels.

Even more, the proclamation or reading of the Gospels is a true sacrament of the presence of the spirit of Jesus among us. To read the Gospels with the attitude of a disciple is to encounter Jesus. Together with the Eucharist, reading the Gospels constitutes the most intense experience of Jesus in the life of the Christian.

We are interested here in contact with the Gospels in relation to spirituality and as a norm for following Jesus. Because it is impossible to completely treat all aspects of this here—all Christian spirituality is evangelical, based in the Gospels—we will treat only the evangelical aspect that best synthesizes the message of Jesus' spirituality: the discourse on the Beatitudes. The Beatitudes are the summary of the Gospels' spirit and the Word of God as the way of human perfection.

## *The Gospel of the Beatitudes*

It has been said, with greater or lesser truth, that Jesus' Sermon on the Mount (or the group of discourses so named) is a summary of gospel spirituality. It is perhaps the most popularized of Jesus' discourses, and the one that has had the greatest influence. We can consider the Beatitudes to be a synthesis of the Sermon on the Mount and of the spiritual values that Christ taught us.[1]

Jesus himself is an incarnation of the Beatitudes. Lived and proclaimed by him, they become the spiritual values of a Kingdom that is primarily Jesus himself. The Beatitudes are the "great prophecy of the Gospel," precisely because they propose an ideal that is completely unattainable on earth but that at the same time into which we might grow. It is the ideal of the "new person" who is clothed in the spirit of the Gospel, clothed in Christ.

The prophetic character of the Beatitudes also carries

with it the impossibility of being lived without the special presence of the Holy Spirit because the Beatitudes surpass human effort. They presuppose the gift of wisdom, strength, and the delicacy of love that the Spirit grants. Therefore, the Beatitudes are prophetic and little understood. If on the one hand they are worthy of admiration, even among nonbelievers, they must also give rise to a certain skepticism and incomprehension. They demand more-than-human effort and can be misinterpreted. They can be a source of scandal and an object of ridicule. We may judge them as being inappropriate. We must always remember that although the great demands of the Gospel—such as forgiveness, nonviolence, celibacy, poverty, and even the Beatitudes themselves—are always open to ridicule, they are within the spirit of the Gospel and within the limits of human understanding.

Faced with this reality, the Beatitudes remain the great message of Christ to his disciples. The Gospels are precise in recording that Jesus speaks to his disciples—that is, to those who in some way will be different. He speaks to Christians, involved in a dynamic of becoming new people. He also speaks to disciples who, on the one hand, desire evangelical perfection and who, on the other hand, seek happiness. Jesus does not place human happiness in opposition to gospel perfection. We are so much made for happiness that we cannot find in Christ's demands, including the Beatitudes, a contradiction of God's call to happiness. Christ has made the two coincide and promises us gospel happiness in the present time. The Beatitudes are not only a promise for another life but are a promise and light for the present. They are not a consolation; they are not alienating; they are at the same time eschatological and historical. The Beatitudes keep us from the danger of living a pregospel or intertestamentary spirituality in order to overcome purely human ethical norms and the spiritual ethic of laws and commandments.

We know that the Gospels bring us two complementary versions of the Beatitudes: Luke's and Matthew's. Luke's version (6:20–26) teaches us who is blessed (or challenged) objectively in the Kingdom that is offered us. Luke tells us that the Kingdom has a preferential option for disciples of a certain social status (the poor, the hungry, the afflicted, and the persecuted).

Matthew, however, has a more specific preoccupation with respect to Christian spirituality. He tells us how we become blessed (whatever our human and social status is), what basic attitudes we should cultivate to share in the Kingdom, and what attitudes identify us with the spirituality of Jesus. Matthew's Beatitudes (5:1–12) synthesize the style of spirituality according to the Gospels.

There are eight Beatitudes in Matthew. In the "middle eastern" style of the Gospels and Jesus' discourse, we understand that these eight Beatitudes are mutually inclusive, diverse facets of a single basic message, enriched and developed in a spiraling fashion. The richness of angles that Matthew's version of the Beatitudes gives us makes each of us feel called to live some more intensely than others. But we know that if we take seriously the demands of one of the Beatitudes, we also advance in the others because they incarnate the same message. The one who is truly poor according to the Gospel is also meek, merciful, committed to justice, and so on.

## The Sacramentality of the Church

Jesus' humanity lived through the Spirit was and is the single radical source of Christian spirituality. As such, and owing to the historical way in which Christ chose to remain among us, the sacramentality of the Church—expressed in the sacraments and particularly in the Eucharist—is a primary source in all spirituality.[2]

It is commonly said that one of the difficulties of the contemporary spiritual quest is the need for and importance of sacramental practices. A crisis exists in the valuation of the sacraments and their meaning for Christian life and works. Despite a relative devaluation of sacramental participation, many Christians and Christian communities have evolved and profoundly transformed their vision of Christian commitment and life, and are coming around: they are seriously seeking the sacramental dimension of Christianity and its mysticism. They have understood that the Christian life—indeed, human life—is deformed without a sacramental, symbolic, and ritual dimension.

There are complex reasons for the devaluation of sacramental practices. For the most part it is a reaction to the excessive and ingenuous sacramentalism of the past few centuries. Christianity has been weak in terms of conversion and evangelization, as well as in its demands for transforming an unjust society according to the Christian faith. The irony of sacramental and celebrational Christianity in a sinful society has awakened doubts about and reactions against the historical relevance of sacramental practices.

While popular religion and its sacramental practices have been looked upon with suspicion by "progressive" pastoral leaders, Christianity has drifted toward a more secularized form, in which "religious" aspects of faith and the Gospel (such as sacraments and religious practices) have been devalued and greater emphasis has been placed upon "secular" values (such as the commitment to transform reality, social struggle, and the option for liberation). It is still too soon to achieve a balance in this movement toward somewhat elitist characteristics, but ultimately a new equilibrium should be sought as well as a synthesis of both the elitist and popular viewpoints.

Finally, there has been an equal emphasis in pastoral activity on the evangelizing value of collective liberation and how historical liberation relates to the anticipation of the Kingdom of God. This is a valid goal of evangelization: to move from an emphasis on private conversion and realization of the Kingdom to insist on historical and collective conversion and the realization of a just society as the presence of the Kingdom. The temptation is to undervalue the coming of the Kingdom as personal conversion, as an exodus from the sins of the heart, as the way to sanctity. And so it is not easy to find meaning in the sacraments and their efficacy. Efficacy seems to be measured only in terms of the struggle for a better world. In the face of this, it is necessary to reaffirm the primary importance of the sacraments in pastoral work and spirituality, seeking a new synthesis that avoids the pitfalls of the past and the present.

This need is supported by a fundamental truth: the primary source of spirituality and the values of the Kingdom is not the reality of the secular world, but rather of Jesus Christ. He alone is the way, the truth, and the life, for the human condition as well as for faith. Christianity as well as human liberation is founded upon, in its most radical aspect, following Christ (Jesus as truth and way) as well as participating in the life of Christ (Jesus as sanctifying and liberating life).

Jesus is the life and source of all life, and spirituality is life. In our surrender to Christ, his liberating life is given to us. This theme is as central to the Gospels as is the theme of discipleship, especially in the Gospel of St. John (see the parable of the good Shepherd, the discourses to Nicodemus, to the Samaritan woman, in Capernaum, at the resurrection of Lazarus, at the Last Supper, and so on). In John, Jesus is light, life, living water, the bread of life, that we might have his life. The root of Christian spirituality is sharing in the life of Jesus, in order to follow him.

Yet Jesus, his life and liberation, is found primarily in the Church as sacrament. The Church is the original and privileged sacrament of Christ offered to society as life and liberation. In a certain way, there is only one sacrament—involving Jesus and his Kingdom—and it is the Church. Every life-giving presence of Jesus is a sacrament, and this presence is given globally to us in the Church. The Church—as sacrament of Jesus—is incarnated and made concrete within the human condition and daily life, made explicit in the various sacraments of the Church such as the Eucharist, penance or reconciliation, baptism, the liturgy, the saints, the Word of God that shapes every sacrament, and so on. The individual sacraments are not isolated; they are the expression of the global sacramentality of the Church as the sacrament of Christ. The community of the Church is expressed in each Christian sacrament; each Christian sacrament encapsulates the life and liberating grace of Jesus.

We know, however, that in Christian spirituality, what we call the sacraments of the Church (word and rites) are not the only experience of Christ and his grace. We know that our neighbor, the poor, and the community are also presences and experiences of Christ and his liberating grace. They are authentic places for Christian spirituality. But if the neighbor and the poor can become, for the believer, an experience of faith and fellowship, it is because the believer has already encountered Christ as the source of faith and love, present in the Church, through its word and sacraments. If the neighbor, the community, and the event are for the believer an encounter with Christ, a Christian experience, it is because in reality it is a re-encounter, an actualization of the experience of Christ already realized in some way in the sacramentality of the Church.

Catholic theology teaches that the sacraments of the Church are a privileged encounter between ourselves and Christ. The liberating and sanctifying Kingdom of God is offered to us with special efficacy in the sacraments, in which Christ is present in a privileged way, for various reasons. We will dwell on these reasons here.

*The sacraments embrace the fundamental dimensions of human life and experience.* In fact, human experience is not simply a day-to-day thing—it is not simply what in Christian terms amounts to the daily presence of God and his Kingdom in life. Human experience—all human experience—is punctuated by intense, radical, and critical moments that appear on the path of life. It is in these moments that, at least implicitly, one experiences the transcendent, mysterious aspects of life and the consequent limitations and precariousness of the individual and of history. This is the basis of what is called religious experience, the religious dimensions of the individual. Although many people react irreligiously to these experiences, or give them a nonreligious interpretation or response, the experience of the precarious and finite, while at the same time mysterious and transcendent, is an inescapable and inevitable occurrence.

This "limit experience" becomes most clear in the great crises in the life of the individual person, especially at times of birth, death, surrender to love, experience of evil and sin, of solidarity and fellowship. Therefore, the sacraments respond to these crucial life experiences, to what is at the root of the limiting and transcendent experiences of life.

Through the sacraments, the fundamental experiences of each individual are embraced and interpreted through Christ and his illuminating and liberating action. They are transformed into genuinely Christian experiences and, as such, into fully human ones. And while the sacraments make the human condition of Jesus of Nazareth and his liberating death and resurrection present and tangible in the heart of the individual, they at the same time proclaim and ensure that radical human experiences such as death and suffering have been liberated and redeemed by God and have reached their true spiritual meaning.

Jesus and his Church assure us that simple and ordinary symbols, rites, and words, celebrated and shared in the Church with that conviction of faith, are efficacious; that the experience of guilt and sin is liberated and sanctified in the sacrament of penance or reconciliation; that the experience of love's intimacy is humanized and recovers its full meaning in the sacrament of matrimony; that one's birth is also an entering into the life of the Kingdom of God through baptism; that illness and death, through the sacrament of the sick, have been transfigured and, because of the suffering and death of Christ, are the decisive purification of our entire being in view of the resurrection; and finally, that the painful human search for fellowship, justice, and love, in the Eucharist is embraced by Christ and transformed into a certain promise.

*The sacraments are an encounter with the living Christ.* In the Christian sacraments, the symbolism of life that is communicated is always given beneath the sign of an encounter.

The effect that the sacraments have on us is the most authentic form through which we encounter Jesus today. It is the same effect that took place in Jesus' encounter with his disciples in Palestine, at the Last Supper, with Mary Magdalen at the banquet, with the blind and the lepers on the roads of Galilee, with the good thief on Calvary. "All of the people tried to touch him because power went out from him which cured all" (Luke 6:19; Mark 3:19; and so on).

Because the sacraments are encounters with Christ in the biblical sense—that is, an experience of faith, of love, of imitation, and of sharing in his transforming life—they are in and of themselves liberating and sanctifying, showering upon us Christ's mercy. According to the Gospels, to encounter Jesus is itself a liberation from misery and sin. When Jesus explained the forgiveness of sins, he stated that it had already taken place in the encounter with him (Luke 5:20; 7:48).

Jesus' transforming mercy present in the sacraments is offered to us as growth in faith, love, and life according to the Spirit. For example, the sacrament of matrimony is an encounter with the life-giving love of Jesus, whose symbol is the mutual surrender of two persons who love each other and who want to make that love their life project. In its sacramentality, this encounter is sanctified and consummated by Jesus' love for humanity (the Church), which gives to matrimony its fidelity and strength.

The same is true of penance or reconciliation. The

symbol is the encounter of the merciful Jesus with the sins and miseries of a human person. In its sacramentality, this encounter of the penitent with Jesus of Nazareth who forgives and purifies is as efficacious, tangible, and real as Jesus' encounter with Mary Magdalen or with the paralytic, whom Jesus liberated from their sins. In every case, the encounter with the sacrament of reconciliation, either private or communal, transmits to us the liberating life of Jesus in the form of his mercy, the forgiveness of sin and guilt, and the gradual purification of the roots of our slavery.

In the Eucharist, the symbol is an encounter of brothers and sisters who in fellowship celebrate the death and resurrection of Jesus. In its sacramentality, Christ becomes part of the community and communicates his life of radical love to it, encouraging it to struggle for the cause of the Kingdom and its justice, to the point of the sacrifice of the cross in the hope of the resurrection.

In summary, the sacraments are a liberating and sanctifying encounter in such a unique and radical way that there is no substitute or any other parallel—personal, social, psychological, or political—in human liberation. They change and liberate the root of our life, where freedom, the choice between good and evil, selfishness, and love are played out, where the essential orientations of existence are decided. They change and liberate the "limit experience" of the human person, including the experience of guilt, evil, and sin, where the fact that life and death are mysteries is revealed and where the finality of a life that is not in our hands reveals our radical limitation and poverty.

Where does this radical efficacy of the sacraments, as symbols of the encounter with Jesus, come from? It comes from the very profound fact that every one of the risen Jesus' actions upon the world and upon persons (through the sacramentality of the Church) is a paschal action. The life that Christ gives to us in the sacraments is a paschal life: we die and at the same time are renewed. We die to evil and sin to live according to the Spirit in a process that spans the entire path of our life, which is also the path of spirituality.

The paschal life that we receive in the sacraments is also the gift of a promise. In each sacrament we are given eternal life as a participation in the present and as a hope for the future. The sacraments are signs of total liberation because they are signs of full paschal life.

The same symbols that the Church uses in its rich sacramentality signify the encounter with a life that gives life: bread, wine, oil, water, light, and others. Each symbol contains a form of encounter with the life of the paschal Christ and symbolizes the triumph of this life over the reality of our death.

*Spirituality has a sacramental dimension.* The experience of the sacraments is essential as a source of Christian spirituality, because faith encounters in them all of its vigor and all of its ecclesiality. The sacraments presuppose the experience of faith but they also nourish it and cast it in its communal dimension. In the Church's sacramentality we celebrate in common our spiritual experience. Christian spirituality, in a word, is a sacramental spirituality.

We say that this spirituality is sacramental because the sacraments mark its path and accompany the most intense and crucial moments of its journey, from initiation in baptism to the rites of the dead. In a special way, the two repeatable and habitual sacraments—Eucharist and reconciliation—are the most powerful and ecclesial moments of the Christian life.

The sacramental dimension of spirituality, placing the experience of faith in objective reference to the life of Christ present in the tangible and visible signs and words of the ecclesial community, prevents spirituality from becoming subjective, individualistic, or losing its identity. The sacramental dimension of spirituality has its fullest meaning precisely in the fact that the sacraments nourish spirituality like water nourishes the grass. Life according to the Spirit (also called the life of grace) has its richest source in the sacramental signs.

It is the constant and certain teaching of the Church that the sacraments are the source and experience of grace. It is true that the liberating grace of Jesus is given to us in many ways, in events, in the commitment to a greater love, in secular and social values, because the Spirit blows where it will. But in the Church's sacramentality, grace becomes tangible, guaranteed by apostolic tradition conserved by the Church today, and particularly intense and liberating. The sacraments are the favored places for grace.

What is the significance of the grace that the Church gives to us? First, grace means what a person receives from God as unearned and gratuitous. Human life, the vocation and meaning of a person's existence, the task to liberate both oneself and society, are all experiences that surpass pure human ability, will, and aspirations. All of this is something mysterious that is given to us. Human experience illuminated by faith tells us that we are more than we are, that we are called to the life of God, which we cannot reach by ourselves. The deepest part of the human person, his or her human life as well as the life according to the Spirit, is received from God as free and unearned gift, as grace. God takes the initiative and priority in our life.

The mysterious giftedness of the human condition, at its deepest levels, is appreciated above all in the higher experiences such as friendship, love, unselfish surrender to a cause, tragedy, evil, suffering, and joy. In all of these experiences there is an element of gratuity, of undeservedness, of mystery that surpasses every purely earthly effort and that is open to a transcendence that is beyond the individual.

These realities are proclaimed, remembered, and communicated by the sacraments, which are signs of God's free and transforming intervention in our life. The sacraments give ultimate meaning to the mystery of life as a life of grace. Furthermore, by the sacraments we are permitted to live these experiences in all of their fullness, as true human beings, in the way of Christ and through the strength of his grace.

Second, grace has to do with the intimate relationship with the Absolute, with God to whom the individual is called. This eminently liberating relationship grows and is deepened as we are clothed in Christ and live as children of God. It is precisely grace, whose home is the sacramentality of the Church, that is the primary source that clothes us in Jesus, making us "new creatures" and gradually liberating us from all sin and alienation, transforming us into children of God. Grace is the life of Jesus within us that makes us his followers. All of this surpasses our own efforts and possibilities; alone we cannot suppress sin nor can we live like Jesus. All of this requires the free intervention of God's liberating love in our lives. This intervention comes to us in a privileged and visible way in the sacraments, the historical form of our encounter with Jesus, the only certain and trusted sign of our vocation to fullness and intimacy with God.

The dimension of the gratuity of human life and commitment (even in historical tasks, authentic liberation is given to us as a gift) signified by Christian sacramentality, is difficult to comprehend, and even more so to live, in contemporary Western culture, which is characterized by an overvaluation of immediate and measurable efficacy and by productivity and pragmatism. For this reason there is difficulty in integrating the sacraments with work and daily struggles, with their own dimension of grace, gift, celebration, and radical liberation of every human life. The temptation is to make the sacraments (especially the Eucharist) only a launching pad for action and commitment, or a religious device to jog the conscience of activists. This perspective, with other preoccupations, prolongs the purely moralizing vision of the sacraments.

But the meaning of the sacraments in spirituality, as we have already described, is much more profound and decisive. God cannot be manipulated, cannot be reduced to our own challenges and tasks. The Christian God, "God with us," is not only help and life but should be recognized and loved for himself. This attitude, aptly expressed in the Christian prayers and sacraments, is profoundly liberating for us; we are humanized as long as we let God be God, free and unmanipulable, and as such capable of letting the person be fully him- or herself, free and unmanipulable in turn.

Perhaps the difficulty we have in accepting the sacraments as merciful gift and grace from God stems from the extreme difficulty of accepting the goodness of God and his grace, without merit on our part, and his liberating salvation as freely granted gift. God is not an accountant or a foreman; the most profound experiences of Christian spirituality are sanctifying and liberating due to the pure goodness of God (Matt. 20:1–16).

The sacraments not only give us the energy of Christ for our struggles and commitments (although this much is true), but even more they proclaim and offer as grace the fact that our struggles, commitments, and all of human reality are already redeemed and liberated by Christ. The sacraments are not only the celebration of life, but the celebration of a redeemed life. They are not only the celebration of the struggles of a people, but are the celebrations of Jesus' embracing these struggles and being present in them as the source of efficacious hope.

The sacraments are the signs that crystallize and incarnate the mysterious alliance (covenant) between God and freedom, God and history, in our spirituality. Freely given grace as God's liberation as well as the freedom, tasks, and struggles of humanity are condensed in the sacraments. Because of this, spirituality has a sacramental dimension that helps to resolve the great tensions of Christian experience; for example, the tension between the gratuity of grace and the efficacy of human tasks, and the tension between struggles and commitments and the need for feasts and celebrations.

The sacramentality of Christian spirituality responds to the multidimensional character of human existence, which includes personal fullness (sanctification), struggle and commitment, contemplation, and politics. The sacraments in human life help us avoid the dehumanization that stems from the cultivation of only a few of life's dimensions. They remind us that the only dimension that is included in all human experiences is the experience of faith. Neither politics nor sexuality nor economics is an all-inclusive dimension of human life; each is a fundamental dimension that includes others, but none includes all of our vital experiences. That is the privilege of the Christian experience, which in the sacraments achieves an always dynamic and incomplete synthesis between the experience of faith and the diverse experiences—political, familial, loving, and celebratory—that Christians live.

The sacraments are necessary because they are the favored place where we most fully receive and experience the fact that God is the radical source of our activity, our commitments, and our choices. These are also a gift from God. We are made to recognize that God is greater than our heart, that our struggles are in his hands, and that life is entirely colored by his mercy.

### *The Eucharist and Penance*

In the ordinary practice of spirituality, the sacraments we habitually share are reconciliation or penance, and the Eucharist, which is the sacrament of our encounter with Christ par excellence.

Everything we have already said about the sacraments is verified in the Eucharist, but in a special way. In fact, all of the other sacraments lead to the Eucharist, because the Eucharist is not only the sacramental presence of the spirit of Christ; it is the real presence of Christ. The Eucharist is not only the application in the Christian community of the paschal dynamics of death and renewal; it is the sacramental celebration of Easter itself, the sacrifice of Christ, with its grace of death, renewal, and participation in the life of the Spirit, made sacrament in the heart of the community. The Eucharist not only transmits the life of Christ to us; it enables us to commune concretely with Christ himself, who transforms our life into his life. The Eucharist is not only a grace of love and surrender to others, a fraternal grace for the community that celebrates it; it is the renewal of Christ's love for and surrender to the Father and to us, and it carries the entire community with him in this surrender. Christ's presence in the Eucharist is that of a "surrendered body" and "blood that has been shed."

We are not mistaken when we say, with the Church, that the Eucharist is the most important source of Christian spirituality, one for which there is no substitute, for it concentrates all of the other sources of the Spirit. The Church continually exhorts us to nurture and awaken our faith in the Eucharist, sharing in it as often as possible.

The Eucharist and penance must have a balanced presence in Christian spirituality. This has not always been the case in Church history. In the past, participation in the Eucharist has often been limited (considered a type of spiritual "luxury"), while penance has been continually advocated. More than a sacrament, penance has been seen as a devotion. In fact, throughout history, it has often substituted for the Eucharist in Christian practice. But in the present day, we are seeing a reverse trend. The Eucharist has been revalued while penance has fallen into disuse. Now the Eucharist appears to substitute for penance.

The truth is that the two sacraments should be equally present in Christian practice, without substituting for one another. It is true that, in itself, the Eucharist is more excellent than penance and that the Eucharist should be attended more often than penance. However, participation in the sacrament of reconciliation cannot be ignored or postponed indefinitely; if so it is at the risk of losing a very significant dimension of spirituality.

In the sacramental structure of Christianity and salvation, Christ made penance the full and decisive vehicle for reconciling the individual with God. It is where conversion to God and reconciliation with him and with others becomes a real event in our lives. In penance, we concretely and sacramentally repent and are converted to God, and Christ concretely and sacramentally receives our conversion and bestows his grace of love and mercy upon us.

In penance, the life-giving and paschal encounter with Christ takes on an aspect of forgiveness and mercy. It is true that we can—we must—continually repent and ask forgiveness of God outside of the sacrament of penance. But these repentances by nature converge toward the sacrament of repentance and forgiveness, where reconciliation is fully confirmed and where the encounter between misery and mercy becomes a salvific and ecclesial event.

The sacrament of reconciliation, furthermore, involves another special grace: the grace of dying with Christ. As in no other experience of conversion, the Holy Spirit identifies us with the death of Christ, which for us means dying to selfishness, sin, and to the deep tendencies toward evil that remain within us and that only the Holy Spirit can overcome.

But we also know this through experience: authentic participation in penance is always a return to the beginning, a strengthening of our spirit to overcome faults and temptations, and it is a very profound spiritual experience of the encounter with the merciful face of Jesus.

### Sacramentality as the Structure of Social Grace

We Christians today speak of social sin, institutionalized sin, sinful structures. What this means is that in contemporary society and culture the diverse forms of violence, the growing distance between rich and poor, labor injustices, the margination of the vast majority of persons, social and racial discrimination, and the abuse of women and children are all dehumanizing sins that are not perpetrated only occasionally or in private, but that are systemic, predominant, and public. These sinful situations are generated by social, economic, and political institutions themselves and are reinforced by the predominant cultural mentality and by administrative corruption. The gravest thing of all is that this institutionalization of sin leads to quieting of consciences, to despair, and to loss of dignity, especially—but not exclusively—among the poor and oppressed. The structures of social sin are manifested not only in situations of poverty, but also in modern wars, genocides, concentration camps, the situation of immigrants in wealthy countries, racism, and in many other forms.

It is in the context of these diverse facts that we experience today as social sin or the structures of sin—from the concentration camps to the Bolivian tin mines—that we can better understand the meaning of the sacramentality of the Church and the liberating grace that it contains. The sacraments are the nemesis of social and structural sin. Grace appears in the sacraments as the structure of hope and liberating grace.

Let us explain. Personal and private sins and injustices do exist. Like all sin, these are liberated by the grace of Christ, which leads to personal conversion. On this level, the confrontation between sin and liberating grace is hidden in the mystery of freedom. The social repercussion of this kind of sin, although real (because every sin affects others in some way), is not always structurally and socially dehumanizing.

Social sin, the "sin of the world," however, causes collective and massive dehumanization; it creates public and historical signs of social despair and oppression. This is why it has received so much attention in the contemporary Church. Sinful structures are the most severe forms in which the sin of the world is seen today. This sin includes not only socioeconomic sins but also sins against life, against the family, sins that corrupt love and sex, the sin of the arms race and of the dehumanization of technology, and the like.

In the face of these sinful structures, private spirituality and purely personal conversion are not sufficient to reveal and make real the liberating grace of Jesus, who wants to transform not only the interior of the person but also the social structures of the world. Therefore Jesus' salvation places structures of grace in opposition to structures of sin; social grace is opposed to social sin. Social grace—the structures of grace—are given to us in Christian sacramentality.

The sacraments are the visible, efficacious, and hopeful signs that reality consists not only of structural sin, but that reality is also decisively interjected with structures of liberating grace. But his liberating grace must become visible and experiential, because the reality of the structures of sin is supremely visible and oppressive. In the sacraments, the grace that crosses social realities is made visible and is collectively experienced. This is why the sacraments are able to maintain a collective hope, as well as human dignity and conscience, in the midst of evil.

The subject of moral evil, the sin of the world, and original sin is important to Christianity as well as to any human experience. The doctrine of original sin (the sin of the world) is well known: we are joined together in sin. The original root of sin, selfishness, and injustice is in the human heart, in society, and in history. This assertion is not only a truth of faith. It is also historically verifiable: evil, selfishness, the exploitation of humans by humans, are a permanent reality, inseparable from the human condition. One of the more evident expressions of this is the structures of sin. Sinful structures are not rooted in any particular economic, political, or cultural systems, because they always reappear in new ways in new systems. The structures of sin have a single root in the evil that we call original sin. The evidence of this evil is too universal and notorious for this evil to be ignored.

Yet original sin is not the center of the Christian experience. The central focus of Christian faith—which in turn influences the entire experience of history—is Jesus Christ and the redemption and liberation that he brought us. It is an elementary affirmation of faith that with his resurrection, Jesus liberated us from sin, once and for all. This liberation lives on in the risen Christ, who with his liberating grace "gives light to every man coming into the world" (John 1:1ff.). Christ's spirit acts today in the roots of history, the human heart, and society, producing a dynamic of grace contrary to the dynamic of sin. We call this original liberation.

### Original Liberation

Because of Christ, there is in the human condition a solidarity of grace and fraternity, and not only of sin. Original sin ceases to be the protagonist of history. All human persons are in solidarity with one another not only in evil and sin but more deeply in the liberating grace and spirit of Christ.

Even more, we believe that the radical liberation that Christ offers us is stronger and more definitive than the sin of the world, because grace is stronger than sin. St. Paul reminds us that "where sin abounded, grace superabounded," telling us that original liberation, and not original sin, is the decisive reality of the human experience.

But it seems as if this were not true, because very often the strength of sin is dominant, and the statement that human beings are radically liberated appears to be weak in the face of experience and visible evidence. The explanation of this is also sufficiently wise: every human person must be converted, must embrace and actualize the liberating grace within himself or herself. Original liberation is the path for following Jesus that is called spirituality. Original liberation is not automatic; it must be accepted. For it to be accepted it must be recognized, experienced, and have sufficient historical visibility for it to be socially recognized.

The root of sin emerges in history in structures of sin. The root of liberating grace emerges in structures of grace. Hidden and private grace is not enough, acting only in the human heart to express the fact that the radical liberation of Christ is already on the road and offered to all. Nor is it enough to express the fact that this liberating grace is present in history and society in a stable and experiential way. Liberating grace requires structures of grace that efficaciously proclaim that the sinful structures are already conquered at their roots.

These structures of grace are the sacraments, the sacramental structure of Christianity, the sacrament of Christ present in the Church, in the community, in the pastors, in the Word, in the signs of grace, in the Eucharist... Christian sacramentality is the liberating grace that rises from the oppression of sin. It is structured grace, cultivated in the desert of evil.[3]

In the sacraments, love and fraternity are offered to us as the ongoing structure because hatred and division are the permanent structure of sin. In the sacraments, forgiveness and reconciliation are offered to us as the structure of grace because sectarianism and cruelty are the structures of sin. In the sacraments, the Kingdom is offered to us as the structure of grace because exploitation and injustice are structural. In the sacraments, love and mercy become visible structures because evil is visible and structured. In the sacraments, liberation is given to us as a structure of grace because slavery is structural. Life is given to us as the seed of grace continually offered to all because death reaches every corner of the human condition. The sacraments are the present of our future. They are our hope and desire for goodness and liberation made present because despair is the temptation of present evils.

## The Witness of the Church

The sources of spirituality that spring from the spirit of the risen Christ, who lives in the Church, are not exhausted by the Word and sacramentality. The Spirit that acts in the ecclesial community also raises up living witnesses to the faithful and heroic following of Jesus. These brothers and sisters of ours are the saints and martyrs that the Church offers us as the ideal of Christianity and as inspiring witnesses of spirituality. The saints—and not only those who have been canonized but all of the followers of Christ who throughout history have given authentic witness of the Christian life in their communities—were and are for us a source of mysticism and spirituality.

## *The Saints*

For Christianity, the saint is the incarnation of the ideal to which the Church pushes and guides us but is rarely realized itself among us. Within the profoundly human symbolism of Christianity, the saint is the symbol of the gospel life, envisioned and placed within the reach of all people, showing us the way to follow Jesus in various cultural and historical contexts, the way to live according to the Spirit in diverse junctures and challenges.

The saint is the living commentary of the written Gospel. He or she is the proclaimed Gospel in the life of a person who was, like us, open to sin, temptation, and the search for God in faith.

When the Church considers someone to be a saint, it identifies with that person. This means that the Church declares that the individual incarnates authentic Christianity and that he or she can be imitated as a source of spirituality. In this sense, the Church is not identified with bishops, or popes, or theologians, or activists—unless they are saints. In this sense, the Church is holy; it is infallible in administering the sources of sanctity and in proposing the examples of this holiness.

Thus the Church has two ways of identifying authentic Christianity: in its spiritual teaching and tradition, through which it guarantees the truth of the ideal Christian (orthodoxy); and in proposing saints, through which it guarantees the truth of Christian practice (orthopraxis). The lives of the saints incarnate that which the Church proposes as true Christianity.

The living witness of the saints is carried on long after their death. The saints are a living reality in the Christian community. We can relate with them. They can be our friends and companions on the path of our life. This communion of saints, which on our part is expressed as devotion to the saints, is before all else a communion of love and a grace of imitation. Devotion to the saints is deformed when we see them as a substitute for Jesus, or as supermen or superwomen who did not live the same lives as ourselves or who have heavenly powers that are the sources of miracles, rather than seeing them as a source of inspiration for our following Jesus.

Among all of the saints, there is only one who represents a universal and necessary devotion. Only one incarnated the life according to the Spirit with absolute fidelity: Mary, Jesus' mother.

### The Virgin Mary

We are not going to speak here of Mariology but rather of Mary's relationship to Christian spirituality.[4] Given this perspective, we cannot touch upon the enormous variety and richness with which the devotion to Mary has been clothed in the Christian tradition and in the experience of a believing people.

We want to recall the fundamental facts in which to root any authentic devotion to Mary. *Mary is the perfect incarnation of Christian spirituality.* It is in this sense that the Church calls her the archetype of the Christian, or the model of the Church. Mary is the perfect follower of Jesus, from the annunciation of the angel to the foot of the cross. Mary lets herself be led, unreservedly, through the life of the Spirit; she is filled with the Holy Spirit (Luke 1:35).

Mary lives her fullness of sanctity as a normal creature. That is, she walks in faith, listens to the Word of God, embraces it in her heart, and is absolutely faithful to it

(Luke 2:19, 51, and so on). She lives according to the spirit of the Beatitudes to the point that the Gospels call her the great blessed one, for all generations (Luke 1:45, 48; 11:27–28).

The absolute fidelity of Mary is woven in the midst of perplexities, darkness, and conflicts appropriate to faith (Luke 1:34; 2:19, 41–51). Like Jesus, she experiences temptation and the cross (Luke 2:35) and through them she identifies, unlike any other disciple, with the mission and redemption of her son, Jesus.

The privileged position of Mary in the Church and in spirituality springs from her total fidelity to the Word and the plan of God. For this reason, she remains the best model for those who wish to learn to be Christians.

*Mary signifies the presence of the maternal love of God among us.* We know that Mary is the mother of Christ and so the Mother of God. She is the mother of the Church for each and every Christian. She is the mother of all humanity. Mary is our mother through the Holy Spirit, and this divine maternity is the source of her graces and privileges; it is equally the value that qualifies her role in the Church and Christian spirituality.

In being the disciple of Jesus and his follower like us, Mary is our sister and companion. In being the mother of Jesus and our mother, she is the efficacious symbol of the maternal love of God toward us. In her we experience in a particular way the feminine aspects of God's love: his delicacy, tenderness, emotional closeness, depth, and mystery. It is true that God's love revealed in Jesus Christ is the same, with or without Mary; but from our point of view, given that we can only perceive that love in a human and sensitive way, God has also made use of Mary as mother and woman to help us understand his love.

If our spirituality were to lose Mary's feminine and maternal touch, it would run the risk of being dehumanized, of losing the affectional and spontaneous quality with which it is clothed. Mary assures that the Church itself is a warm family because it is part of feminine charism to create life and friendship. Mary, the sign of the feminine face of God, helps also to liberate the Church and its spirituality from the rigidity and rationalism that often threaten to extinguish the life of the Spirit.

*The special graces and privileges of Mary are for us the hope that the life of Christ within us might someday enter into its fullness.* We know that Mary has special graces; she is preserved from all sin, even at her own conception; she is carried into heaven immediately after her death ... These extraordinary graces often distance us from her and make her appear to be someone apart from our race and human condition.

Yet authentic Christian spirituality never dehumanizes Mary, just as it never dehumanizes Jesus because of his divinity. Even with her special graces, Mary is also our sister: she lived those privileges in the ordinariness of the life of her time, in the poverty and obscurity of Nazareth, and in the darkness of faith.

Even more, her extraordinary graces will one day be shared by all of us, her brothers and sisters, once the path of spirituality, after death, reaches its destination in the resurrection and the vision of God. We are also called bodily to heaven; we are also called to an absolute purification from all sin. Mary has preceded us and so, for us, she is a sign of hope that those promises of God will be fulfilled within us. Mary is thus the model of our future life.

*The revelation of the maternal face of God in Mary*

*makes her especially present in the spirituality of the poor and oppressed.* It is among them that her feminine mercy is revealed and embraced in all of its significance. In spirituality, Mary is the mother, sister, companion, and the hope of the poor. From her appearance in the mestizo face of Our Lady of Guadalupe, Mary has been adopted by the people as a sign of Christian hope and liberation. The poor and suffering of our earth sense, in her, the loving solidarity of the God of the poor and the justice that raises up the lowly and casts the mighty from their thrones (Luke 1:51–55).

### Love for Our Brothers and Sisters

Love for our brothers and sisters—our neighbors—is a final indispensable source of Christian spirituality. All of the previously mentioned sources of the Spirit and Christian life would be deformed if they did not lead us to the practice of fraternal love. The decisive proof of our following of Jesus and that we are living according to the Spirit is that we love our neighbor (1 John 2:7–11; 4:7–16).

Moreover, love for our neighbor is a source of spiritual experience not only because it is the best verification that we are living according to Jesus' spirit but, above all, because the neighbor is the privileged "place" for our encounter with and experience of God. Loving our neighbor, we love God, and our surrender and service to that neighbor out of a greater love are the basis for an authentic spiritual experience.

Because God is revealed as Father of all people and Jesus, identified with each one of our brothers and sisters (Matt. 25:40), my neighbor is for me a sacrament of God;

in my neighbor's face I encounter something of the face of Jesus. And because God is revealed preferentially as the God of the poor, and Jesus wanted to identify preferentially with them, the face of Jesus is especially encountered in the face of the poor.

Fraternal love and service to the poor as sources of Christian spirituality are of such importance that an adequate presentation would surpass the limits of this chapter. We will return to this subject in order to treat contemplation and commitment (Chapter 4), fraternity (Chapter 5), and the meaning of the poor (Chapter 6). For now, it is enough to point out that love of neighbor is a special effect and source of Christian spirituality.

### REFERENCES

1. J. Dupont, *Las Bienaventuranzas* (Lima: CEP); Segundo Galilea, *Spirituality of the Beatitudes* (Maryknoll, N.Y.: Orbis Books, 1984).
2. John Paul II, *Dives in misericordia* (Rich in Mercy), 1980.
3. Cassiano Floristán and L. Maldonado, *Los Sacramentos, Signos de Liberación* (Madrid, 1978); Segundo Galilea, *Renovación y Espiritualidad* (Bogotá: Indoamerican Press, 1981), Chapters 8 and 9.
4. *Puebla Documents,* nn. 282–303; Paul VI, *Marialis cultus,* 1974; Leonardo Boff, *El Rostro Materno de Dios* (Madrid: Paulinas, 1979).

# 3. Christian Conversion

## The Struggle Against Evil

God the Father calls all persons to follow Christ, led by the Spirit. Our response, which is Christian spirituality, begins by faith, which animated by love unleashes conversion.

Christian conversion is the firm decision accompanied by appropriate means of placing us on the path of following Jesus. Conversion is always a break, a change, a change of mentality: we begin to be guided by the criteria of faith and the Gospel and not by the criteria of the world and the flesh, closed in on ourselves. Conversion is a change of practice and attitudes: we begin to act in imitation of Christ and not out of selfishness, idolatry, and passion. More profoundly, Christian conversion is a rebirth, according to the life of the Spirit, that clothes us anew in Christ.

Christian conversion is an initial decision and crisis (break), but it is also a lifelong process that accompanies following Jesus. In this process of growth there are crises, new decisions, and rupture—all powerful moments in life. The path of conversion is the path of every individual spirituality.

### Sin and Blindness

The first decision and consequence of conversion is the overcoming of sin, at least conscious sin. Sin is the only reality incompatible with life according to the Spirit and with any spiritual progress. Therefore, the first condition of Christian life is struggle against the sin and evil that are in each one of us. In this struggle we count on the sources of the grace and liberation of Jesus that the Church offers to us.[1]

Sin is the ultimate human evil. Not only does it impede us from following Jesus, but it also dehumanizes us, making us less human. What is worse, grave sin—as the deliberate and total rupture with God, our brothers and sisters, and with ourselves—puts us in danger of radical dehumanization and condemnation.

We must also struggle against small sins and infidelities. They weaken our moral strength, our capacity to overcome, and our decision to follow Jesus. They desensitize us to the great human and Christian values and to the actions of the Spirit. They make us comfortable with the spirit of the world, ignoring our gospel criteria, making us vulnerable to acting according to the flesh and not according to the Spirit. Finally, they deprive us of true interior peace.

Blindness is one aspect of our condition as sinners. Blindness is not a deliberate sin, but it is linked to it: it is the highest form of spiritual insensitivity. Blindness is not seeing or not perceiving our egoism, our faults, the points we need to overcome. The sinner is also blind, not perceiving the evil within. To go out from sin is first to see. Conversion begins by becoming conscious, by seeing the light.

We are responsible for our blindness, at least indirectly, for our negligence in seeking out the means to attain light that is contained in the sources of spirituality. Unconscious sins, acts of omission, the incapacity to overcome crisis and temptation, have our own blindness as their near or remote cause

It is not surprising, then, that the salvation that Jesus brings to us appears very often in the Gospels as liberation from blindness and as sending light. Christ appears as the light that disperses the darkness (John 1:4–9; 8:12, 31ff.). He comes to give sight to the blind (Luke 4:18; 7:22; John 9:1ff.).

In his "woes" to the rich, the satisfied, and those who laugh (Luke 6:24–26; 18:24), Jesus deplores the condition of the rich and powerful, and the difficulty of their conversion, not because they are necessarily sinners but because they are blind. They do not see where their true riches lie; they do not see the needs of others; they do not see the implications of their faith. To be converted and to follow Jesus is to gradually be freed from all our forms of blindness.

### *Temptation*

The struggle against evil and the work of conversion never ends because the tendencies and roots of egoism and inner blindness are with us until the day we die. These roots and tendencies—sin latent within us—want to surface in ever-new ways; they want to seduce us to evil and infidelity.

Temptation is neither sin nor evil but only its means of seduction. In this sense, Jesus himself knew temptation because it was not incompatible with his absolute holiness. Temptation is part of the human condition that Jesus assumed, except sin (Luke 4:1–13; 22:39–44).

Temptation is thus a normal condition of the Christian life. No one—even those in the highest stages of spirituality—is exempt from every form of humbling temptation. To not want temptation is a subtle form of pride. The struggle against temptation is the most ordinary way we struggle against evil in the process of our conversion.

The Gospels portray the temptation of Jesus as coming from outside (the devil in Luke 4:1–13) or from his human condition as such (Luke 22:39–44). In Jesus there were no interior roots or tendencies toward evil; in ourselves these roots and tendencies are the fruits of original and personal sin. We have those roots that the spiritual masters identify as the desire to possess (things, wealth, pleasures, persons... ); the desire for esteem (various forms of vanity, prestige... ); the desire "to be" (the basic egoism that substitutes for God and fraternity... ). Temptations can continually arise from these roots as substitutes for the gospel way of channeling those tendencies, when we act according to the flesh and selfishness, the sources of sin.

The struggle against temptation is the struggle for being, valuing, and possessing according to the humanism of the Spirit.

### Christian Abnegation or Self-denial

Beyond the question of sin, Jesus presented Christian conversion and commitment as self-sacrifice, as self-denial, and as daily taking up one's cross.[2] For him, the path of the Spirit is a kind of combat, doing violence to us, entering by the narrow door (Matt. 7:13; Luke 9:57–62; Matt. 10:25–36; 11:12; 16:21–24; 17:15; John 12:24–26).

Christian spirituality has a dimension of death and abnegation of the "old man" in order to live according to the Spirit of the "new man," even after having overcome sin. The spiritual tradition of the Church has called this dimension Christian asceticism.

Abnegation or Christian asceticism goes beyond the mere renunciation of evil and sin, which could just as well be the object of a natural asceticism or any healthy humanism. To simply renounce evil is not Christian spirituality; Christian spirituality goes beyond this. It leads us occasionally to renounce even the legitimate in order better to imitate Jesus and seek an always greater God.

Christian asceticism as the renunciation of legitimate values is the most specific aspect of Christian witness. In renouncing even these values, we reveal the eschatological nature of human life that points to higher values. Renouncing the legitimate, we give witness to our faith in the values of the Spirit and to our hope in the coming Kingdom as the only absolute value.

Christian asceticism has many valid motivations, beginning with the vocation to follow Jesus and not only live a natural ethic, a vocation that stems from the love that wants to be identified with the life of Christ. This motivation was common in many saints who renounced even the good and legitimate so as to be better able to imitate the arduous and sacrificial life of Jesus Christ.

A second motivation comes from the reality of temptation and the tendency toward evil within us. We need to maintain control of these tendencies (diverse in every human being) and the freedom to seek the greater God who calls us always to be more than we are. We need to balance what is unbalanced in each of us. To do this, at certain times and in certain situations we must "act against" (St. Ignatius), renouncing the legitimate to recover our balance and freedom. Gluttony is more easily overcome with a period of fasting; egoism, with concrete and free commitments in service to others.

Following St. John of the Cross, we should also add

that asceticism and renunciation are necessary to purify the "darkness" (blindness) and "attachment" (lack of freedom) that impede our being attuned to God in order to experience him through faith. The experience of God demands not only not sinning but also purity of heart. Given the human condition of inadequacy to experience God through faith, we need to purify this faith. This purification is attained through the path of asceticism.

Yet any ascetic motivation ceases to be Christian and human—and becomes stoicism, a simple exercise of will, or a form of pessimism toward human possibilities—if it is not animated by the imitation of Christ due to a love greater than ourselves. Asceticism is not Christian if it does not humanize us, if it does not free us, if it does not make us grow in love. Let us look at some examples.

Poverty as a material or sociological lifestyle is not of value in itself. There is no greater Christianity in living in a poor house and neighborhood than in living in one less poor. The lack of things is not a special perfection, and spirituality has nothing to do with having or not having things. In and of themselves, things are indifferent or neutral. Moreover, those who voluntarily live among the poor know that their material poverty is a very relative witness, that in relation to the poor that surround them, they are privileged, and their efforts at poverty are dubious and unclear for these people.

Material poverty, however, is a Christian witness not because of its materiality, but because of the motivations and greater love that it reveals, and through the energies of commitment and solidarity that it is capable of arousing. What makes poverty a witness is not the lifestyle itself but the fact that through love someone wants to share the situation of the poor, their struggles, and—as much as possible—their level of life. Material poverty is a dubious gesture; but it is always valid in the context of a spirituality that reveals the sincere search for a greater love and imitation of Jesus.

Another form of renunciation of the present day that is called into question is that of the consecrated celibate. On the one hand, it is traditional in Christian mysticism to say that consecrated celibacy is a spiritual value and a witness. On the other hand, many celibates—and noncelibate believers—do not seem to find special value in celibacy.

What is the case is that, as in any other form of renunciation, the consecrated celibate who is isolated from greater love is certainly not a witness on a path of spirituality. The fact of not being married or of not having intimate sexual relations is not in itself a perfection or a special gospel value.

But the consecrated celibate who lives within a context marked by the living out of a greater love *is* a witness. It is not the mere fact of not marrying (material celibacy) that gives witness (in this sense, they are right who question material celibacy in many cultures), but rather the evangelical motives that are made clear in this option and the quality of commitment and fraternal love that give rise to this option for consecrated celibacy—is a significant witness not so much in its materiality but through the spirituality that it supposes and generates. Consecrated celibacy is an experience of the fact that God is real, that his greater love is real, that he is a source of greater love for others, and that all human love is relative to the absolute love of God.

Let us also consider the traditional renunciation of penance. Penance involves all the self-denials and sacrifices, accepted or sought, through which we express our purification and escape from sin and evil tendencies. Ancient spirituality gave great importance to penance; acts of penance were systematically undertaken in daily life and physical penance was emphasized.

It is hard for us to understand this today, but that way of penance was meaningful to a certain culture in terms of a certain model of sanctity and the prevalent anthropology (characterized by attitudes such as pessimism toward the body and a spirituality influenced by monks and religious with little value placed on profane activity). Nevertheless, penance as a witness of Christian spirituality continues in its essential value as a form of sacrifice of egoism to live for a greater love and to imitate Jesus.

The cultural context of Christianity has been transformed in modern times. Today one speaks less of sin and more of selfishness, of alienation from our being, of idolatry of sex, wealth, and power, and so on. We no longer consider the body to be the source of sin and the enemy of the spirit. Today we do not like penitential acts programmed, systematized, and added to our daily life. Christian life today is not grounded in the contemplative-cloistered ideal; it values profane activity and temporal works as Christian duty and the source of self-denial.

But in our cultural context, penance is effective as a demand and an inescapable dimension of the interior life if that life wants to be committed to a greater love. Primordial penance is seen first as the demands—demands that have as much to do with attitudes as with physical sacrifice—that spring from Christian commitment. One would have to say the same thing about the self-denial imposed by family life, matrimony, daily work, and so on. The self-denial that life itself demands is transformed into

Christian asceticism as long as it is motivated by love and relates us consciously to Jesus' call to follow him "carrying our cross every day."

In summary, devotion to any cause requires discipline, ascesis, abnegation. For a Christian, this is the new face of penance. Penance is life embraced without egoism and in a plan of love. Part and parcel of this is the cross that we must carry every day. For Jesus, this is the proof of a greater love.

## Conversion as Process

We said that conversion is process and growth, always unfinished. The fact that the Christian vocation is not merely turning away from sin but rather living according to the Spirit makes conversion an ongoing task.

The process of conversion is neither homogenous nor linear. There are critical moments, decision points where we must again choose Christ; and conversion passes through the crisis of maturation and growth. All of this forms part of the "purification of the depths of our spirit to prepare us for God" (St. John of the Cross), in such a way that the experience of faith and the motivation of love become the dominant factors of our spiritual journey.

The more mature conversion is, the more it is guided and motivated by faith and less by enthusiasm, sensitivity, felt generosity, or the consolations of the Spirit. One needs to learn to grow and develop through the various stages and crises of Christian conversion. This leads us to rediscover and continually choose the values that attracted us at the start, under the new light of a more purified faith which, as such, is more arid and dark to the senses. In the mature Christian life, conversion is allowing ourselves to be led by the Lord of faith, of the cross, and of hope: "I tell you solemnly: as a young man you fastened your belt and went about as you pleased; but when you are older you will stretch out your hands, and another life will tie you fast and carry you off against your will" (John 21:18).

### Conversion as Human Maturity

Spirituality, it must be remembered, has close ties with psychology. The Christian path—conversion—is also the path of psychological maturity.[3] The experience of faith, hope, and Christian charity, and the gradual activity of the Spirit also contribute to the maturity of the human faculties, without substituting for the autonomy of the psyche. While the grace of God's love impregnates the faculties of the Spirit, the psychological organism is also humanized.

Spirituality in itself does not resolve psychological problems or imbalances (not all of the saints were psychologically healthy) but as long as it integrates psychology with love and pulls it out of egoism, it helps us to live in peace with ourselves and even to make psychological conflicts and limitations a path for further growth.

Our human growth—which is also our Christian growth—is achieved through our growth in love. From this perspective, Christianity is a reordering of our human values in terms of love. Love is the axis of our life around which we mature psychologically.

We must grow and mature in every aspect of our human and Christian life, from biological, intellectual, and affective maturity to the maturity of faith. There are certain psychological areas where maturity is more difficult to achieve than in others, and where the experience of faith can contribute significantly to our maturity as human persons.

For example, there is affective maturity. This is not easy to achieve and comes about through a long and arduous path, owing to its likeness to the maturation of love and Christian charity. On this point, Christ's commandment to love coincides with the process of affective maturity. Affective maturity is the capacity to give of oneself over and above the need to receive. It is the capacity to accept, without being frustrated or diminishing that which is given, nonresponse to our love and surrender. It also is the capacity to be objective and emotionally detached in situations, to judge correctly and justly.

Another form of maturity where there is a close tie between psychology and grace is social maturity. This refers to our capacity for integration and authenticity in relation to diverse types of persons, groups, and situations. The mature person feels accepted and accepts others as they are; he or she is authentic without pretensions or complexes. The socially immature, on the other hand, are revealed by their aggressiveness, complexes, conflicts, and maladjustment.

We said that it is not enough to mature in only one area; it is necessary to grow in all of them, within a dynamic where psychology and grace maintain their autonomy yet remain as two inseparable dimensions of the call to maturity and Christian conversion.

Therefore, we do not reach maturity upon the ruins of our psychological tendencies but upon their proper orientation and purification. Our tendencies are radically good and salvageable, and they form a part of our human/Christian personality. We are not speaking of overcoming them but of organizing them around love, which is the axis around which all maturity is constructed.

## The Social Dimension of Conversion

As we have already said, Christian conversion is the starting point for spirituality. It is the process of choosing Jesus and his Gospel. It is Christian because we are converted first to Christ and through him to justice, love, neighbors, the poor, and the Kingdom of God. Christian conversion is conversion to a God who is inseparable from the love of neighbor.[4]

In practice, the preceding statement seems problematic. The problem revolves around one of the objections that religious and sacramental practice encounters—namely, that there are too many practitioners whose conversion is incomplete. Faith in practice certainly influences some aspects of life (personal, conjugal, and family ethics, honesty in the workplace and in business), but too often it does not influence other areas of life that seem to be impermeable to the dynamic of conversion. We are referring to the well-known cases of sincere and practicing Christians who are reactionary in political, social, and economic matters, who are more or less unconsciously class-conscious or even racist, who discriminate against others for their ideas or political leanings, who are steeped in the social prejudices and criteria of the class to which they belong.

This leads us to make the point that to be Christian, conversion must also be social. This means that within conversion's global scope, it must break with the sin and selfishness found in each age and place. Thus a Christian cannot shy away from the moral teaching and orientation of the Church. The Church, in every place and time, points up the temptations, idols, and sins that need to be overcome in the process of conversion.

## Conversion and Culture

We have already mentioned the influence that cultural models have had on Christian spirituality. We saw how cultures shape spirituality and how differences in cultures are often one of the causes for the many different schools of spirituality. We also saw how the influence of cultures on spirituality is not always positive and how the cultural context does not always facilitate a greater Christian identity or conversion.

The dynamic of conversion must take a critical distance from its cultural context in order to break with the attitudes, norms, and criteria that are incompatible with the evangelical life. That means that conversion implies a cultural dimension. Although in and of itself, a culture is not converted, men and women within a culture are converted and they, in turn, transform their culture for the better, as long as they are conscious of the cultural implications of Christian conversion.

Conversion to Jesus Christ is also a cultural conversion. What does this mean? What does this have to do with the problem of justice and the distance between rich and poor, with personal and social egoism?

The idea of culture is all-encompassing. Culture touches upon all aspects of the life of a people; it is the collective mentality of a society that is being created little by little and that powerfully influences the members of that society (culture). As stated in the Puebla documents, this mentality is made up of the "values that animate it and the dis-values that weaken it, of its criteria and ideas," and is above all the meaning that a people give to the grand questions of life. Little by little, this collective mentality is crystallized in customs, institutions, and a certain moral sensitivity, different in every culture.

The cultural dimension is of utmost interest to Christian conversion because cultures influence the mentality and ideas that people have of the Christian religion itself, of morality, and in particular of justice and human fraternity; these are all essential values for the Gospel.

Expressing itself in a culture, Christian faith is influenced by that culture and may take on perverting tendencies and elements. This is the case, for example, in Hispanic "popular" Catholicism (in the so-called popular cultures) and in "bourgeois" Catholicism (belonging to the upper class in socially advanced societies). In these cases, religion is enculturated, and an authentic conversion requires of these Christians a purification of cultural deformities.

These cultural deformities manifest themselves, first, in what is emphasized in or left out of the idea of God and Jesus, the Gospel, the Church, the sacraments, and spirituality. According to the collective mentality (culture), God, the Gospel, and the Church are perceived as having to do with intimacy, with the interior, with salvation, and with other-worldly realities, or they are perceived as tied to natural and primary needs of the individual. Purely divine power is accentuated in Jesus, the Church, and the sacraments. The Gospel and the Church are perceived as a religious authority that is either legitimating or subversive, according to the specific culture. One either accepts or rejects the social consequences of the Gospel, and so on.

The influence of culture is sufficiently well known so

that for our objective it is enough to point out here that the conversion to the God of the Gospel, unmanipulable by any cultural or social or personal interest, implies a need for purification of the cultural deformities of specific Christians and the Church. This is better appreciated when we become conscious of the deformities of Christian morality that have occurred due to the weight of culture. In Christian ethics, certain aspects are accentuated while others are played down because of criteria that are more cultural than evangelical. In some cultures, Christians are strict in terms of family and individual ethics and lax in public and social ethics, while in other cultures they are strict in terms of the morality that emanates from law and discipline and lax in terms of human rights. In some cultures, great emphasis is given to sexual morality and little to the ethics of the use of wealth and the rights of the weak, while in other cultures the reverse is true. If Christian conversion is also a conversion of moral customs, these insufficient cultural norms need to be liberated and reconverted to the norms of the Gospel in all of their wholeness.

An important example of the enculturation of Christian ethics can be seen in the deformation of the idea and practice of justice. There is a close relationship between justice and culture: cultures tend to condition, limit, manipulate, and even corrupt the practice of justice. And those people within that culture—even the Christians—if they are to progress in their conversion need to break from and leave behind the prejudices of their culture about justice.

Justice is giving to each his or her own and to all that which belongs to them, without discrimination. This ideal is accepted by all cultures, but is relativized and conditioned in practice by everyone. The fact that there are privileged and deprived social classes or groups—that the rich have the right to more and the poor, to less—goes against the Christian idea of justice. But it happens that these situations have come to be a normal part of many cultures. By cultural custom, the rich do not feel themselves privileged and the poor do not feel victimized, because neither group achieves a true cultural conversion that makes them see the unjust elements of their own mentality.

A conversion to pure justice in individual relations is not enough. Justice is also sociocultural, and the dynamic of conversion must reach this area. Christians must not only question their personal life but also the culture in which they live, that leads them not to perceive collective injustices, such as differences in salaries and earnings, differences in neighborhoods (some receive all services while others do not), and contrasts between luxuries and necessities. Christian conversion is not enough if it does not perceive these injustices.

Another example of the enculturation of Christian ethics has to do with fraternity. Christian conversion must lead to making each neighbor a brother or sister—without regard to nationality, race, social class, or political ideology. But cultures create—each one in its own way—national, racial, class, sexual, and ideological prejudices that make Christian fraternity a caricature or something limited and sectarian. Racism or classism divides society because of a cultural mentality and not only due to a conscious option made out of ill will on the part of people (although this does indeed exist). In the same way, nationalism is a cultural fact and not a personal choice. Some people are able to overcome differences of class or race but continue the sin of ideological discrimination through political ideas, political parties, plans for society, and so on.

All of these divisions cannot be explained simply by a structural analysis of the economy that deals with classes of rich and poor. Ideological prejudices, racism, and machismo are found in all social classes. Even among oppressed people one can find racism and the exploitation of women.

To be converted to fraternity implies leaving aside the cultural roots of antifraternal prejudices in order to live a boundless love. At first sight, racist or classist societies (of any ilk) do not perceive themselves as antifraternal, given that the idea of fraternity itself is stratified; people *do* tend to be brothers and sisters, but within their own cultural milieu. To leave this aside is conversion; to confront the social organization of a culture with the gospel message is to evangelize that culture.

With regard to the enculturation of Christian ethics, we also have the case of liberation (liberty or freedom). All societies preach the freedom of their members (at least as a movement that is under way). The ideal of human rights has a particular role in this. The achievement of freedom and human rights (especially for the poor) are constitutive of Christian conversion and acceptance of the gospel message. But the result is that the same idea of what constitutes freedom and human rights is conditioned by the cultures and ideologies that enforce it.

Cultures influenced by liberalism (capitalism) are sensitive to individual liberties in the face of power but they tend not to be sensitive to economic or labor rights. These capitalistic societies, which are very sensitive to the human rights of individuals in public or private, are socially and culturally insensitive to the economic and social rights of everyone, especially the weak. Marxist and collectivist cultures are sensitive to the rights of labor, of the rights of the majority, and economic rights, but they are insensitive to the themes of religious freedom, individual freedom in the face of the dominant ideology and power, and the rights of dissidents.

This enculturation of the ideals of justice, fraternity, and freedom is further aggravated by the explanations and justifications (ideology) that cultures generate to justify even their limits and deficiencies. When these ideologies are propagated on a wide scale they constitute a manipulation of individual consciences and even of the cultures themselves—a greater injustice.

Nothing of all this, however, has to influence the conscience and freedom of those who share in the society and culture. Faith transcends everyday reality as well as the freedom of the human spirit, which is capable of converting its conscience and freeing itself not only from its egoism and personal crises but also from sociocultural slavery. This gives rise to the possibility of living as Christians in any culture and society, however oppressive and manipulating it may be. The process of conversion, like that of evangelization, has a transcendent and liberating dynamic with regard to cultural and ideological chains.

### Conversion and Sociopolitical Commitment

The experience of conversion freeing us from sin and cultural deformities leads to social commitment: the practice of Christian mercy that desires to better a culture and a society so that others may be converted more easily to the Gospel of justice, freedom, and fraternity. Social commitment is an integral part of Christian conversion where there is the need to build a better society.

Christian conversion is not conversion to a model for society or a sociopolitical ideology, but to Christ and his Gospel. To arrive at social commitment because of him is Christian mysticism. The identity that Jesus established between himself and the Kingdom, with the poor and helpless and with justice and mercy together make the sociopolitical sphere a necessary dimension of spirituality. From the angle of faith, politics is the cause of justice, the cause of the poor. These causes are a consequence of the "preferential option for the poor," inherent in faith. The Puebla document points out that this option requires a "conversion of the Church," and that it is a sign of the credibility and authenticity of evangelization. It is legitimate to add that it is also a sign of the authenticity and credibility of Christian conversion and spirituality.

Moreover, the social demands of conversion are inherent in the very nature of conversion because of the ideal of fraternity that Jesus brought and for which he gave his life. The Christian experience is the experience of fraternity and the commitment to build fraternity between all people. Christian fraternity supposes an economy, a culture, and a politics that make it possible. Fraternity places demands upon institutions and the social order. It requires sociopolitical action, the politics of justice and of service to those excluded from fraternity. For many believers, the call to fraternity (Christian mysticism) becomes a political call.

Conversion to justice and to the poor as integral to Christian conversion requires some vehicles. These vehicles include the programs, ideologies, organizations, or means of action by which the believer opts for better service, in his or her understanding, to the poor. But in these cases, spirituality for the believer is not a program or an ideology, but the mysticism of surrender to the poor out of love for one's brothers and sisters—the greater love that is reflected in the chosen mode of commitment. The experience of faith makes us grow in that surrender, through love and not through a precise ideology.

Becoming conscious that the experience of faith includes the commitment to justice and the cause of the poor has become one of the most powerful themes—both critical and enriching—of spirituality. Today we legitimately speak of the political demands of Christian conversion and of the relationship between prayer, the sacraments, contemplation, and the struggle for justice.

### REFERENCES

1. St. Ignatius of Loyola, *The Spiritual Exercises* (Chicago: Loyola University Press, 1951), First Week; Karl Rahner, *Spiritual Exercises* (New York: Christian Classics, 1966).
2. St. John of the Cross, *The Ascent of Mount Carmel*, ed. E. Allison Peers (New York: Doubleday, 1973); Martí Ballester, *La Subida al Monte Carmelo Leída Hoy* (Madrid: Paulinas, 1970).
3. Segundo Galilea, *Contemplación y Apostolado* (Bogotá: Indoamerican Press, 1973).
4. Segundo Galilea, *Renovación y Espiritualidad* (Bogotá: Indoamerican Press, 1981); CLAR, *Cultura, Evangelización y Vida Religiosa* (Bogotá: Indoamerican Press, 1981).

# 4. The Experience of God

## Christian Contemplation

The process of Christian conversion, of the purification of the spirit and the experience of faith, leads us to and prepares us for the experience of God. This is the central teaching of St. John of the Cross's *Ascent of Mount Carmel*.

The experience of God—in Christian contemplation of God—is a profound, loving, and hidden intimacy (through faith) with the living God. In contemplation, the spirit of Jesus acts powerfully and efficaciously within us, causing us to grow in the life that makes us like Christ. The experience of God is more profound the more alive is the faith and love that produces it, always within the limitation and darkness belonging to the light of faith.[1]

To contemplate God is to experience him in the reality of our life. It is the living conviction, experienced vaguely in the depths of the spirit, beyond the senses and rationality, that the God of Jesus Christ is present within us, in others, and in history as well as nature. It is to experience this presence as merciful and liberating. To contemplate God is to know vividly that we are in his hands.

The contemplative is one who has a living experience of the God of Jesus, who is being emptied of his or her egoism, pride, and the idols of the heart. Contemplation purifies the heart, and the conversion and purification of the heart prepare one for contemplation.

In Christian contemplation, what is important and decisive is not so much the effort that the individual makes in seeking God, through mental exercises or concentration (more appropriate to Eastern forms of contemplation), as it is the action of the Holy Spirit who acts and prays within us (Rom. 8:26ff.). Above all, to contemplate is to let oneself be loved by God.

An equally important characteristic of Christian contemplation is its incarnate and committed nature. It is nourished in life, action, and especially in all forms of fraternal love. This is so because according to the biblical revelation, the Christian experience of God has two fundamental "places": the person of Jesus himself contemplated in prayer, and the neighbor, service to whom out of love is equally an experience of Christ ("As often as you did it for one of my least brothers, you did it for me" [Matt. 25:40]). These two ways of encountering and "seeing" God enfold the double dimension of Christian love ("Love the Lord your God with your whole heart . . . and your neighbor as yourself") and the ways that Jesus is revealed to us according to the Gospel ("I am the way, the truth, and the life"; "What you did to my brothers you did to me"; "Whoever does not love the brother he does see, how can he love the God he cannot see?").

The call to experience God is a call to grow in friendship and to surrender to Jesus in prayer, and a call to learn to encounter him in the service of fraternity. There is no authentic Christianity or contemplative experience if we do not cultivate both demands and if we do not seek their synthesis.

This leads us to establish once more the deep relationship in Christian spirituality between contemplation and commitment. The fraternal dimension of Christian contemplation allows commitment through love to our brothers and sisters to be an experience of God and that experience to be translated into commitment.

## Christian Prayer

Prayer is the most eminent and irreplaceable form of the experience of God.[2] All of the characteristics and demands of Christian contemplation must be applied in a special way to prayer:

—Prayer includes us in the prayer of Christ to the Father, "since he forever lives to make intercession" (Heb. 7:25) for us, and through that prayer we begin to share in the experience of God himself in his humanity and in his redemptive activity. Through prayer we follow the praying and contemplative Christ.

—Prayer is not perfected through mental technique and effort (as useful as this is as part of the method of prayer) but through the life according to the Spirit who prays within us. The Holy Spirit is the protagonist of Christian prayer.

—The path of prayer supposes the path of conversion of heart and the search for love and self-denial. At the same time, prayer purifies the heart and pulls us away from idolatry and blindness.

—Prayer is a dark and often difficult and arid experience of God. Such discouragement in prayer is akin to the Dark Night of the Senses on the level of faith that leaves one unsatisfied and in semidarkness in terms of the senses.

—Christian prayer is supported in the experience of God by life and action, leading to commitment.

The experience of prayer requires the practice of prayer. There is no spirit of prayer without its practice. Here we are referring to prayer in the proper meaning of the word: human activity through which we relate to God in an exclusive manner. "We think of God loving him" (St. Teresa). We are also referring to all forms of prayer: private, communal, sacramental, and liturgical. The different forms and methods of prayer have essentially the same characteristics and demands—that is, the loving response to the love God has for us.

In discussing the concrete practice of our prayer, we enter into a tough and problematic area for every individual. It seems that we do not know how to pray (Luke 10:1). It seems that we do not encounter God, that we are distracted and bored. Our prayer suffers from constant negligence, distractions, and crises. Sometimes a change in activity or lifestyle is enough to weaken our prayer. Our prayer seems unproductive, fragile, and vulnerable.

All of this should not surprise us, because it is the nature of prayer to be typical of the experience of faith. Without the conviction and motivation of faith, prayer is neither understood nor practiced. Prayer is one of the few activities that we achieve purely through faith and purely because of God. Being an experience of faith, prayer is dark and frustrating to our normal way of being and acting, which puts all of the sense and intellectual faculties into play. Yet, in prayer, the Spirit works upon the "foundation of the soul," upon faith and love, leaving us in the void of the senses and of the human way of doing things.

In this sense, prayer is a rupture or a break in order to enter the level of faith and the exclusive relationship with God, who is always greater than our heart and our reason. Therefore, the practice of prayer may be "violent." It demands of us a certain violence, an option of faith. Except on very rare occasions, prayer is not easy or spontaneous; it requires a renewed choice every day. As an option, as "violence," prayer is similar to other gospel practices that also go against the grain: celibacy, forgiveness of offenses, the option for the poor, and so on.

In summary, prayer is problematic, because it is the activity that is most dependent on our life of loving faith. Faith is not prayer, but in the reality of the human condition prayer is like a thermometer of faith. We do not pray out of mental or emotional necessity. Many Christians pray when they feel the need and do not when they do not feel it. But there are many people who do not feel the need to pray and never practice prayer. To wait to pray until the need is felt means to postpone prayer indefinitely. We pray not out of feeling the need but because of a conviction of faith and in order to clothe ourselves in the love of Christ.

The problem of the time we dedicate to prayer hinges very often on the strength of our faith. Growth in prayer is not a question of time; we do not grow in the experience of God only through accumulating a certain number of hours in the practice of prayer. Yet at the same time, growth in prayer is indeed a question of time: we must give time to prayer, to be alone with God. Every Christian, by reason of his or her vocation and contemplative roots, is called to a certain time of prayer. If we are habitually and systematically deprived of this time, we will eventually experience a spiritual and apostolic "anemia," a stagnation of the process of conversion and a weakness in the face of temptation (Luke 22:40–46).

We often have the excuse of not finding sufficient time for prayer. It seems that our work and duties are incompatible with times of prayer. But we know by experience that the question of finding time is one of conviction and values; in this case the conviction and priority of faith. We are able to find time for those things we value and we do not find it for things unimportant to us. Having time is always a question of our scale of values. In practice, it is enough for our convictions about prayer to be weak or wavering for any other activity to take priority.

Above all, we must recognize that modern life and tasks do not facilitate a systematic practice of prayer, even if there is the good will to pursue it. One must learn, then, to pray according to one's own rhythm, which may not always be a daily rhythm. This implies having, at regular intervals, more powerful and prolonged periods of prayer, such as retreats, prayer meetings, and the like. According to his or her own rhythm, the contemplative Christian must know how to reserve those special times when we recover our spiritual, human, and even emotional balance, when we introduce a desert experience into our lives that places us once again in the truth before God and in view of our life and activities. In summary, then, prayer is the one activity capable of returning and maintaining unity in our life that is always twisted and challenged by disparate and disintegrating worries, activities, and tensions.

Is prayer an end in itself or is it a means to invigorate our life and our faith? Prayer is both things at the same time. It is an end in itself because our earthly condition is the realization of the human vocation to live in communion with God, to experience God. Furthermore, prayer prepares us and conditions us for the definitive and face-to-face vision of God.

Prayer is a means because it makes us redeemers like Jesus, through which we influence life and events. Prayer makes us redeemers with Jesus because, like the Lord in the loneliness of the desert, in the garden of Gethsemane, or on the cross, we carry the sin of the world and we liberate our brothers and sisters as well as ourselves from the roots of evil, of selfishness and blindness. On the level of redemption and of clothing us in Christ, prayer is efficacious. On the level of identifying us with the will of God, prayer is efficacious (Luke 11:9–13). Christ has promised us that if we pray constantly, the Holy Spirit will be given to us; our being and acting will be converted, we will grow in the life according to the Spirit and in imitation of Christ. This will happen to us and to those for whom we pray.

But Jesus has not promised that prayer will be efficacious for every need, every desire, and every whim. Nor will it be so in order to realize that which God wants the individual to do with the intelligence, responsibility, and knowledge that God himself has given. Prayer is not a substitute for human responsibility, nor is it a "lifeguard." When we pray for a sick person, for example, the purpose of that prayer is not necessarily that health may return but that the ill one may be identified with the will of God and may live his or her illness as a child of God.

In the spiritual tradition of the Church, we have insisted upon the value and primacy of the faith in the practice of Christian prayer. Yet this should not leave us with a spiritualized and unincarnated idea of prayer. Because of the incarnate nature of faith and because the one who prays is a person who has faith, and not an impersonal faith, Christian prayer also has an anthropology.

In other words, Christian prayer takes into account the concrete person, who is embedded in a culture, with a body, with an existence, and with a being sensitive to signs and words. This anthropological element of Christian prayer has often been forgotten by pastors, not only in liturgical prayer but also in private prayer. So that prayer may touch upon the fullness of a person relating to his or her God, we cannot undervalue postures and bodily attitudes, the intelligibility and emotional value of religious signs, of vocal expressions, of texts that will nourish prayer. All of these elements, which are essential to the liturgy, must not be left out of the teaching of personal prayer. This leads us to certain considerations.

*The problem of our prayer is linked to our way of life.* Lifestyles without any self-control or discipline are psychologically incompatible with activities such as prayer that demand of us the exercise of faith. If our lives do not have discipline, we do not have the freedom necessary for an authentically contemplative encounter with God.

It is in this regard that the evangelical style of our life takes on special value in our struggle against evil, in self-denial and asceticism, and in overcoming temptations. A healthy emotional life, the ability to be silent and to interiorize, to control ourselves and our own actions, also influence our prayer. In traditional spirituality, the contrary is called activism. Thus just as it is well known that we live as we pray, so it is equally true that we pray as we live.

*Another important consideration in the anthropology of prayer is the method of prayer.* This is an aspect we tend to ignore far too often, sometimes in reaction to the rigidity imposed upon and excessive importance attached to prayer methods in the past, especially beginning in the sixteenth century. But method is simply a way of helping us, aiding our faculties to be concentrated on God, making the break between daily tasks and prayer.

The schools of spirituality throughout history have offered and do offer from proven experience a diversity of methods. No one method can be imposed on all Christians because the most appropriate method depends a great deal on each person and the stage of his or her life. From among these methods, we should arrive at one simple and personal method that does not stifle the Holy Spirit and does not weigh us down. The spiritual masters tell us that a method becomes more and more unnecessary the more we make progress in prayer, and that to remain tied to methods and practices when the Spirit has begun more directly to guide and encourage prayer is counterproductive.

Each age has favored some methods over others. Today we readily encourage communal methods of prayer, based on interspersing gospel readings with testimonials, or prayer and shared songs. This method recovers for us the value of ecclesial and liturgical prayer. One should remember that private prayer keeps its value because it corresponds to the very personal way that the Holy Spirit acts within each one of us (Matt. 6:6ff.). In the life of prayer, the Christian must know how to balance communal and private prayer without abandoning either of the two, and to use them in the proportion that is suggested by his or her own spirituality. (Some pray better in private and others in shared or common prayer.)

In any event, we must know that prayer is called to

evolve and progress. Its tendency is to become simpler, to become more and more contemplative and led by the Spirit, to become less discursive and methodical, to evolve toward an experience of God's presence perceived only in the realm of faith and love.

Even in its highest stages, however, prayer has its times of aridity, its accumulation of distractions, its moments of being colored by feelings of our own incompetence. This is because prayer has a great deal to do with the mystery both of faith and of God himself. Jesus has asked us to pray constantly, even in darkness and incompetence, without being discouraged (Luke 11:5ff.). The point of Christian prayer is not so much what we gain or discover as it is what Jesus does within us through his spirit.

REFERENCES

1. St. John of the Cross, *Spiritual Canticle;* Martí Ballester, *El Cántico Espiritual Leído Hoy* (Madrid: Paulinas, 1979); St. Teresa of Avila, *Autobiography;* Rene Voillaume, *En el Corazón de las Masas* (Madrid: Studium, 1962); Segundo Galilea, *Espiritualidad de la Evangelización* (Bogotá: CLAR, 1980), Chapter 9; Thomas Merton, *Seeds of Contemplation* (New York: New Directions, 1986); Leonardo Boff, *La Experiencia de Dios* (Bogotá: CLAR, 1975); E. Tremen, *La Mística Carmelitana* (Barcelona: Herder, 1981).
2. St. Teresa of Avila, *Way of Perfection;* Rene Voillaume, *Cartas a los Hermanos,* Vol. 1 (Bilbao: Desclée de B., 1963); José Comblín, *La Oración de Jesus* (Santander: Sal Terrae, 1978).

# 5. The Demand of Fraternal Love

## Fraternal Love

We have already touched upon the fundamental demand of fraternal love in Christian spirituality. Speaking of the identity of spirituality, we have pointed out that spirituality must be incarnated and that the privileged place of faith's incarnation is in one's relationship to one's brother or sister.

We have also said that the face of our neighbor, particularly the poor and oppressed one, is one of the indispensable sources that nourishes Christian spirituality. In addition we have pointed out that the experience of God is inseparable from commitment to and love of our brothers and sisters, and that conversion to God is equally linked to conversion to the love of neighbor.

We have seen that the demand of fraternal love is translated into the commandment of mercy, proclaimed by Jesus in the Beatitudes, and that the coming of the Kingdom in history takes place in terms of mercy and fraternity.

Christian fraternity is the fruit of fraternal love. As long as charity progresses in the world, in societies, in communities, and in families, fraternity arises. The love that Jesus brought to the world and for which he gave his life is not limited to purely individual relationships but tends to create fellowship, a communion, as a form of relationship in all types of human community.

Through fraternity, Christian spirituality is our response to the grand Utopia of the Kingdom preached by Jesus, the communion of people among themselves, inseparable from the communion of people with God and the human vocation to happiness and eternal fraternity. Likewise, Christian spirituality responds to the ever-frustrated longing of the human spirit, of philosophies, ideologies, and social movements, to march toward solidarity, justice, and fraternity.

### Christian Fraternity—The Spirituality of Community

To achieve Christian fraternity is our challenge.[1] And if Christ's great achievement—and as such, that of Christianity—is the Church, it is absolutely imperative that the *Church be fundamentally a fraternity.* If it were anything else, it would lose its relevance in the world and its credibility would be seriously damaged. If the Church is a fraternity, then in all of its expressions and groupings it must realize the event of Christian brotherhood and sisterhood; if the Church as a whole is not a *Christian fraternity,* it will suffer from not being distinguishable from other worldly or religious groupings.

We have said that the ideal of fraternity is central to Christianity and has been in some way a constant in all religions and social ideologies, even in our day. But together with these diverse ideals of fraternity, which always fall short, the Gospel proposes to us its full, absolutely original, and demanding ideal, to the point that we can say that Jesus' great message was to reveal the ultimate meaning of human brotherhood and sisterhood.

This great message was outlined in Judaic revelation. The Jewish people were a people of brothers and sisters, although this fellowship was limited in practice to those of the same nationality or religion, those who were the children of Abraham (Lev. 19:17). Throughout the history of Israel, God was educating and preparing the people for the wider, more universal fraternity that was often explicitly proclaimed by the prophets (Isa. 66:18). Until the appearance of Jesus, however, the Jewish fraternity was nationalistic and its tendency to universality vague.

The Gospel brought a new ideal of fraternity, so new that in the beginning many Christians—and even some of the apostles—did not understand it. This is the reason for the discussions between Judaizers and Hellenizers, the misunderstandings between Peter and Paul, some people's idea of Christianity as a simple continuation of Judaism.

Misunderstanding the ideal of fraternity was not only a problem for the first Judaizing Christians. It still afflicts the Christian community, always attempting to be more a group of people belonging to a common creed and rite but forgetting that essentially we are challenged to realize the *Christian fraternity as event*. This is why it is so important to reflect upon how Jesus and his Gospel propose fraternity and what its characteristics and demands are. This will help us better understand the concrete demands that fraternal love presents for Christian spirituality.

Christian fraternity is marked by an original event, that Christ the Lord truly became brother to us all. Fraternity as such finds its axis in this fraternal relationship that we have with Jesus.

God's historical integration with the human race through Jesus, the son of Mary, is neither a myth nor an abstract idea. It means that he forever remains our brother (Rom. 8:29) in no way different from his other brothers and sisters (Heb. 2:17). Furthermore, the purely natural basis for fraternity, the human race (which is a vague concept, susceptible to being diluted), is reformed by the fraternal relationship that each person is called to have with the man Jesus, establishing between each one of us a new interpersonal relationship. In other words, we are brothers and sisters because Jesus is brother to each one of us.

However, this fact admits of *varying degrees of brotherhood*. If Christ is brother to all, he is such in a special way to those who seek the truth, justice, and love in their lives (Matt. 12:50; Mark 3:35—"He who does the will of my Father is brother to me ...."). Jesus also has a very original and appropriate fraternal relationship with Christians, his disciples, whom he often called "my brothers" (Matt. 28:10; John 20:17; Acts 1:15; Rom. 1:13; 1 Cor. 1:10). This is one of the dialectical tensions of Christianity; it is why one must realize fraternal charity first with other Christians (Matt. 8:15) and why there is the utmost demand that the event of fraternity begin by being realized within the Christian community.

Christian fraternity rests upon what can be considered Jesus' great revelation to the heart of each person: the fact that the human fraternity has a Father. This is perhaps the fundamental difference between Christian fraternity and all other searches for fraternity. The greatest limit of the latter searches is wanting brotherhood and sisterhood without having a parent. This is at the root of many ideological frustrations and of the drama of atheistic humanism and Marxism. Human fraternity, human solidarity, must have reference to the Father of our brothers and sisters. The idea that there can be no true fraternity without a common paternity and that the common paternity of God creates fraternity is found in the Old Testament (Isa. 63:16), but it is Christ himself who makes this the heart of his message (John 20:17; Matt. 6:9; Luke 11:2; Mark 11:25).

Christian fraternity, therefore, is not simply secular and worldly. The fact of a common Father allows us to hope that fraternity will be realized definitively some day, in spite of human limitations, given that full fellowship is not only dependent on our efforts but also follows from the projection of God's paternity over the human race. The fact of a common Father allows us to overcome all discrimination, because it eases any pretext of distinction or superiority. It allows us to overcome the temptation to live a purely secular and fraternal Christianity because, since God revealed himself in Jesus as Father, every sincere effort at creating human fraternity leads us to the Father (even implicitly) and prefigures the definitive fraternity of all people with him. Finally, the fact of a common Father allows us to rise above the idea that liberation is a purely temporal and political task; rather it is the radical action within history of Christ the liberator, gift of the Father, although it is manifested in a specific place and time.

Beyond all of the values of human solidarity that unite all men and women, Christian fellowship is based in the solidarity of a common faith.

Historically, the human family is created and strengthened by certain human values that create solidarity, such as blood relationship, friendship, a common historical struggle and destiny, common interests and work. This same historical experience teaches us that in many cases, existentially, Christian fraternity involves these values and presupposes them, just as solidarity in Christ is discovered in the historical paths of human solidarity.

Beyond the common values of the human race that inspire the longing for universal community, Jesus made this dream possible by making faith the foundation of Christian fraternity. This brotherhood and sisterhood in faith is not an abstract consensus of doctrines or rites, which experience shows to be incapable of forming fraternity. The faith that the Gospel reveals to us as leaven and dynamic of Christian fraternity is the acceptance of the paternity of God as the magnet of human community, of Jesus as our true brother, and of the message of the Beatitudes as the common inheritance of all Christians (Matt. 23:8; Acts 2:42).

In this sense, the mere consciousness of this faith should be enough, among Christians, to begin on the path toward fraternity. This consciousness can necessarily be strengthened by emotional and social values, but in itself it often has the strength to achieve the event of Christian fraternity. For this reason, for example, in order to celebrate the Eucharist it is not always necessary that everyone present know each other beforehand—although on a psychological level it would be very useful. The same thing can be said of any specifically Christian gathering, as long as a common consciousness of faith in Jesus Christ and his message of fraternity is sufficiently present.

Christian fraternity is not sectarian but is called to universality and communion with all persons and human groups. We said earlier that Christian fraternity is in tension with human fraternity, that the Christian is brother or sister to other Christians and at the same time brother or sister to all people. One aspect speaks to us of what is specific to Christianity, the fellowship of faith; the other speaks of its continuity with the values and desires of the human community and of the universality of the Gospel. To emphasize only the first would make Christianity a sect; to emphasize only the second would weaken the community. Both aspects complement and lead to each other, to the point that if on the one hand Christian fraternity has limits (the common faith), on the other hand the same conditions that limit it demand its universality. What is more, the demand of the common faith that defines Christian fraternity is itself at the service of *all people* in order to better achieve universal fraternity.

The call to fraternal and universal equality is one of the most typical characteristics of any community that wants to be recognized as Christian. Not meeting this challenge has been the cause of failure of many profane and religious ideals of fraternity that have not been able to overcome such barriers as social status, race, or ideology. The Christian community itself can use these barriers as material for an absolutely indispensable and evangelical examination of conscience.

The Christian community or fraternity is not only open to all people (catholicity) but is at the service of all and in some way represents all humanity, just as the "biblical remnant" represents the "multitude," and the leave, the mass of dough. This helps give meaning to the presence of Christian communities, apparently weak and in the minority, among the de-Christianized majority.

Human history—which due to Christ is the history of the liberation and salvation of humanity—is dominated by the idea that this salvation is made possible by a *remnant* (chosen people) selected from among the *multitude* and that serves, and in a certain way represents, that multitude. God saves everyone by means of the historical mission of a few. Without this fundamental criterion of God's intervention in history, it is not possible to understand either the Church or the Christian community.

This is expressed in the story of Abraham, with whom begins the story of the "chosen *remnant*" at the service of all. The people that was born of Abraham—Israel—was minuscule in every sense except the religious, when compared to the multitude of civilizations and peoples of the time. It was a *remnant*. But it had a message, a promise, and an inheritance that in the long run would benefit the entire multitude of peoples on the earth. It is true that in time Israel forgot its universal vocation that its election meant the election of a multitude. It limited itself to a nationalistic and sectarian religion. But within this people there was always a *faithful remnant* that preserved the authentic meaning of Old Testament revelation and Israel's vocation (Isa. 4:3). Saved from the captivity that divided the history of Israel in two, the small remnant—always a minority within a nationalistic and decadent religion—remained faithful to the promise (Neh. 1:2). We can say that before, during, and after the captivity there was a remnant in Israel that kept the promise of universality and from whose womb would be born the Teacher of all peoples.

Christ appeared in history as the realization of the remnant of Israel. He himself, in relation to his time, his people, and even to his disciples—who never finished assimilating him—was a "solitary remnant." His mission is situated along the same lines of Israel's faithful remnant in living and dying for the benefit of the multitude.

Jesus wanted the community of the apostles to be the seed of the Church that would have to continue his work as a remnant. After Jesus' resurrection, each ecclesial community, clothed in fraternity, has been heir to the vocation of the remnant of Israel and of Jesus' surrender "for the salvation of all." This fact must be realized today in every ecclesial community. Outside of this perspective, neither Christianity nor the mission of the Christian in the world—a mission of following the fate of Christ, of being a remnant in ransom for the many (Mark 10:45)— can be understood.

The Gospel hints at the seemingly disconcerting fact that Christians are the remnant in the midst of the world. Jesus referred to Christians as the little flock (Luke 12:32) and as sheep among wolves (Matt. 10:16). He emphasized that "laborers are few in the harvest" (Matt. 9:37) and that "many are called but few are chosen" (Matt. 22:14). Throughout history, demography has reinforced this view, in that the Christian community has never been in the majority with respect to world population, and statistical forecasts predict a relative diminishing of Christian numbers in relation to the growth of world population. Christian fraternity, with all of its demands, has been and is in the minority. But this reality, at first glance discouraging, should not create in us a mystique of failure or a theology of sectarianism or inferiority. It should rather stimulate us to penetrate the essence of a Christianity based on faith, mission, fraternity, and a Church that inherits the mission and fate of the remnant of Israel, of Jesus of Nazareth, and of the fraternity of the Twelve.

In the midst of the multitude, the Christian fraternity is like salt (Matt. 5:13), whose function is to give flavor to food, in the same way as the salt is forgotten in view of the benefit of the food that was tasty. The Christian fraternity is like the grain of wheat (John 12:24) that is not interested in remaining but dies and dissolves in order to transmit its fertility. It is called to lose its life, not to save it (John 12:25), thereby enriching others. Today, the events that are causing secularization in the Church are due to the tendency of a secular society to achieve and proclaim certain values that previously were exclusive to the Christian community, such as the search for peace and justice, public charity, the dignity of women and all races, and education. This gladdens the Church, whose mission is not to monopolize values but to communicate its fraternal characteristics to the world. Instead of deploring these events as competitive with the Christian community or as undermining the influence of the Church, we should contemplate them as a sign that the Gospel is slowly and imperceptibly realizing its mission and that the fraternity proclaimed by it is truly becoming universal.

Following Jesus Christ, the Church and Christian communities are evangelizing the world and transmitting fraternal love not only through apostolic activities but also through the sacrifice of themselves, like the small remnant that represents the masses and that is offered to the Father for the redemption of all. It cannot be otherwise, ever since the time when Jesus saved the multitude once and for all with the surrender of his person. Sacrifice implies the prayer and suffering of the Christian and the community that is incorporated in the suffering of Christ through faith and through prayer. Christian sacrifice is the daily suffering of each person illuminated and transformed by prayer. Thus the Christian community continues the actions of Jesus, whose self-sacrifice represented everyone and opened the way of true liberation for all. The Christian community does not suffer more or less than other communities, but by giving that suffering a sense of mission it is able to represent other communities before the Father and to redeem the suffering of the many, becoming a liberator.

Christian fraternity creates a privileged relationship of brotherhood with each individual or human group that is oppressed or in need, the poor and the "little ones" of the Gospel (Matt. 25:40). The Christian and the Christian community must recognize a brother or sister in every person and act accordingly. Yet the poor and the "little ones" are brothers and sisters in a very special way. That is to say that the presence of Jesus in the poor and the love for them have a primary place in Christian spirituality. The next chapter will be dedicated to this topic.

### *The Mercy That Creates Fraternity*

The Beatitude of mercy calls us to the practice of fraternal love and it shows us the paths of incarnating that love through reconciliation and solidarity.[2] Jesus' teaching, furthermore, reveals to us that the practice of mercy is the only decisive way to create fraternity, making us brothers and sisters of one another beyond our differences. This is the message of the parable of the good Samaritan, the parable of the true practice of mercy and fraternal love (Luke 10:25–37).

Mercy, according to the Gospels, means essentially two things. First, it means effectively acting to help the afflicted and needy, what we call the various Christian commitments to the liberation of the poor and the search for sinners and the abandoned. In the Gospels, the sinner and the poor are the privileged recipients of Jesus' mercy and teaching. In the parable of the final judgment (Matt. 25:31) or that of the Samaritan, we are told of mercy toward the poor and needy; in the parable of the prodigal son and that of the lost sheep (Luke 15:1ff.) we are told of mercy toward sinners.

Second, in the Gospels, mercy is the constant forgiveness of others ("seventy times seven"). The parable of the cruel servant helps us understand that forgiveness is an essential part of mercy and fraternal love, and a condition by which God himself pardons us (Matt. 18:23–35), a condition by which reconciliation and solidarity can become a reality between all persons. Mercy as forgiveness of offenses is the other side of fraternal and united love. If mercy as commitment builds fraternity, mercy as mutual forgiveness and reconciliation rebuilds and strengthens it. Mercy circumvents the division and resentment that offenses produce and that can weaken or paralyze the community.

## The Maturity of Love

Fraternal love has its origin in God, who is love and who loved us first.[3] He spreads his love in us, through the Spirit, so that in each of us who love can grow, mature, and reflect the authentic love with which Christ loved us. If we can love, it is because God communicates his love to us. If we can love, it is due to the death of Jesus through love and his resurrection, which have made love possible.

Jesus' love is the measure of all love. The Christian ideal surpasses the pure humanism of charity ("Don't do to others what we don't want them to do to us; do to others what we want them to do to us") and pushes us to love as Christ loved. This is why the growth of love has no limits in our life and why learning to love is the great, always unfinished task of Christian spirituality. There is often the danger of concentrating on other spiritual goals, other values, and of not giving primacy to the practice of love. St. Paul reminds us that it is useless to surrender ourselves to the poor or to martyrdom if we are lacking in love (1 Cor. 13:1ff.).

In view of the commandment to grow in love, we must remember that we do not know how to love. Our love is a caricature (Rom. 12:9). Our selfishness, our worries, and our sensitivity hold us back. We also know that fraternal charity is the most difficult Christian and human realization—that is, to love as Christ loves, that on earth we will never reach the perfection of love. We know that we fail constantly, that we do not know how to overcome division and resentment, that we are cowards in terms of service, acceptance, forgiveness, and giving something of our life to others. All of this does not mean that we do not want to love or that in fact we do not love. Love is the path of love; loving is wanting to love. What God asks of us, essentially, is not success in charity but the ongoing effort of growing in love and the struggle to learn to love, beginning again each day.

In the struggle to mature in love, the human and gospel dimensions of love walk the same path. There is no separation between human love and Christian charity. The commandment of love that Christ gave to us coincides with the human vocation to grow emotionally, giving over and above receiving and possessing. Jesus certainly widened the horizons and demands of love and gave new motives and a new meaning to them. But his demands for gospel charity are realized and take shape within human love, affection, and the heart, although these are won over by faith and the action of the Spirit (which is why fraternal love is not always sensed and gratifying). We learn to love by following Jesus through love. Once more, he shows us the true practice of love and gives us the light and life in order that we might love as he loved.

What impedes Christian charity is not always conscious ill will, pride, or selfishness. Very often these faults are the result of poor character formation or psychological immaturity, because it is through one's character or psychology that love is communicated. The fact that these faults may not involve sin or be deliberate does not exempt us from having to recognize and overcome them, given the danger that they present in the exercise of love and its communication. Due to a lack of education, an overly timid or distracted temperament may block the dynamic of mercy and the human signs of charity. We may hurt others through distraction or other character faults, often without being aware of it. But aware or unaware, a Christian does not have the right to certain distractions, complexes, or aggressive behaviors that paralyze fraternal love.

There is a part of every human person where temperament and selfishness are more or less mixed together and which is ordinarily left in the shadow. But the love of Jesus must work within us even in those dark areas of our being, even in the unconscious where prejudices, hatreds, and divisions arise. It is true that only in heaven will we arrive at perfect love, but its maturation and growth on the path of life can be attained if we persevere in radical fidelity to the fundamental demand of the Gospel.

### *The Love of Chastity*

Christian chastity is one of the most mature expressions of gospel charity. Chastity is a sign of the maturity of love, and only with difficulty are its demands liberating and humanizing outside of the context of fraternal charity.

Chastity is one aspect of love and thus it is part of spirituality. Chastity is found in celibacy (in which case it is a root aspect of love) or in matrimony, but in every case it is a universal demand springing from the human and Christian ideal of renouncing egoism in relationships with persons of the opposite sex and of fidelity in the commitment of contractual love. For the married person this means loving one's spouse, and for the celibate, loving Jesus exclusively.

The demands of chastity are only understood within the perspective of an always greater love to which we are called and which culminates in the kingdom of heaven, where we "neither marry or are given in marriage" (Matt. 22:30). Within the perspective of fraternal love and the Christian community, chastity means not using the other person. The love of chastity, part of the purity of heart to which the Beatitude calls us, facilitates freedom and openness of the heart, reinforcing fraternal love, its human delicacy, its universality, and its depth. The lack of chastity constricts the dynamic of love.

The chastity to which the Gospel calls us is only possible and only becomes liberating and the source of fraternity if it is consistent with the other values of spirituality and the Beatitudes. The love of chastity presupposes a contemplative experience, and the spiritual tradition has seen a strict relationship between chastity and contemplation ("The pure of heart will see God"), for two reasons: first, because the most profound reasons for chastity stem from the experience of faith and the love of Jesus and his Kingdom, and we penetrate those reasons by the light of contemplation; and second, because chastity is the highest form of the purification from idols and from the blindness of egoism. St. John of the Cross teaches us that the greater the purity of heart, the greater the preparation for the experience of God.

This is why evangelical chastity, and especially celibacy, presuppose a life of prayer, and why prayer, for its part, is so vulnerable to infidelity in chastity. In the same way, the love of chastity supposes the habit of renunciation and self-control. It supposes a healthy and balanced emotional and psychological life. In a word, it supposes a maturity of love such as we discussed earlier.

Because it is one of the original demands of gospel spirituality, chastity—like prayer or poverty—always requires an option of faith. Chastity is never permanent in our life; we must choose it every day and acquire it patiently and gradually throughout our entire lifetime. In this process, we know that the demands of chastity evolve, through different ages and circumstances of life. As with prayer, we must at different stages again learn to love without egoism, learn to endure crises calmly and with fidelity to the love to which we are already committed. Being realistic, knowing our limits, our strong and weak points with respect to chastity, helps us in this. Above all, we must be sincere with ourselves and in our relationship with Jesus, in such a way that there is no resentment in our dark or secret being where Christ's light and grace will not penetrate.

## REFERENCES

1. Joseph Ratzinger, *La Fraternidad Cristiana* (Madrid: Taurus, 1966).
2. Segundo Galilea, *Espiritualidad de la Evangelización según las Bienaventuranzas* (Bogotá: CLAR, 1980).
3. Rene Voillaume, *En el Corazón de las Masas* (Madrid: Studium, 1962).

# 6. The Love of the Poor and Poverty

## The Poor in Christian Spirituality

Love of our poor brother or sister is the proof of fraternal love. The love of the poor—our special brothers and sisters—translated into mercy, solidarity, and the struggle for their just causes, is a constant in the spiritual tradition of the Church. Not only is it an inescapable demand of love, but it is also the source of spirituality and the experience of God.[1]

The traditional—and today, very real—value of the love of the poor, oppressed, and suffering in Christian spirituality has its origin and ultimate foundation in God himself, who has been revealed as a God with a predilection for the forsaken and who has established a particular relationship between himself and them. Thus, the poor and dehumanized of the earth are not only a social reality or a problem that calls for human compassion and justice; in Christianity, the poor are a religious category—that is, having to do with God. To love and serve the poor is to love and serve God; injustice and lack of mercy toward the poor are offenses to God.

The precedents for this religious view of the poor are found in the Old Testament and are especially marked in the prophets of the Exile. We know that the religion of the Jewish people was at that time very centered on worship of God and upon legal and ritual prescriptions. During the Exile, this mentality suffered a crisis because the people found themselves without the possibility of their traditional worship, "no place to offer first fruits" (Dan. 3:38).

The prophets took advantage of these conditions to educate the people in other essential dimensions of their religion (see, for example, Isa. 1:10–17; 58:6ff.). Their message was more or less the following: "It is not so important to have sacrifices to offer because the religion that God wants and the conversion God wants is, before all else, that you be merciful and just to the oppressed, the orphan, the widow, the stranger,... The sacrifice that pleases God is to break the unjust chains, untie the yokes, free the oppressed, share bread with the hungry, house the homeless poor, clothe the naked..." That is, charity to the needy brother or sister, to the poor, has a religious value for God. It is the same as worshipping God. It is the same as being converted to God. Thus the religious dimension of the poor emerges in the Bible. From the description of the Exile on, the meaning of God is understood and expressed more and more in terms of the poor.

All of this is consecrated and deepened in the New Testament. When Mary, expecting Jesus, proclaims in her Magnificat that the salvation of God has to do with justice to the poor (Luke 1:52ff.), she is within the best tradition of the prophets, in line with the "poor of Yahweh," that small remnant that understood and kept their faith in the true Messiah and in the authentic religion as taught by the prophets.

It seems impossible to bring together all of the apostles' teaching about this, and cite how they made Christianity a religion of love of God and neighbor, especially of the needy (see, for example, 1 John 3:16ff.; James 2:14ff.; 5:1ff.).

The religious dimension of the poor remains intact within the Church and has always been taught within it. It is found in the doctrine of all of the fathers of the Church, of all the popes and their most learned magisterium. All Christians know that one cannot please God without having, in some way, what we have called the sense of the poor. It is possible that in certain times and places this teaching has been obscured, especially in preaching and daily life, and that socially the Church may have presented another image. But it can never be forgotten that in the midst of it all, and even in decadent times, the most authentic teaching of the Church has always been the love of the poor as essential to the Christian spirit.

The saints, those Christians whom the Church has recognized as having understood and lived the true Gospel, offer this same witness to us. The saint always has a great sense of God and of the poor. There is no significant saint who has not projected his or her love of God within a commitment, often institutionalized, to the material poor of the day. Certain of these forms of commitment may seem to us today insufficient or paternalistic; these forms were situated in societies, epochs, and cultures that influenced the mentality of the Church and the saints. But what is of interest here is the mysticism of the poor as a special part of the Church's spirituality.

The force of this spirituality in current pastoral activity is a fact that reinforces the religious dimension of the poor as an essential and intuitive part of the Church. Ongoing experience teaches us that when a Christian or group of Christians begins their conversions, when they begin to take their faith seriously, they are soon faced with the problem of the poor who surround them, what to do for them, how to be committed to them, how to share and be in solidarity with them. The actions taken may not always be the most mature and appropriate, but what is important is the religious perception of the commitment to the poor as essential to the journey of conversion. This Christian intuition, universal and fundamental, cannot have any other origin except the teaching of the Gospel, of which the Church is a faithful echo.

## *Jesus and the Poor*

Jesus is the definitive revelation of God as the God of the poor.[2] He is the God who loves them especially, who preferentially brings a Kingdom for them, who exercises his mercy especially for those who suffer the most misery and dehumanization, and who brings justice and fraternity to the most oppressed and ignored of the human family.

Jesus revealed himself as the God of the poor, in that sense, first by his life. He was born to the circumstances of the poor and lived the greater part of his life among them, sharing the obscurity and harshness of a peripheral and scorned town (John 2:46). In his ministry he surrounded himself with simple people, and although he always proclaimed a Kingdom for all without distinction, it was among the marginated, the sick, and the forsaken that he best achieved the signs of total liberation that accompanied his preaching. His death in rejection and abandonment was the final rubric of his identification with the poor. By his life, Jesus preceded his disciples in the preferential option for the poor.

It is well known that the love of Jesus for the poor and oppressed is condensed in his discourse of the Beatitudes of St. Luke (Luke 6:20–21). Stating that the King-dom belongs to the poor, the hungry, and the afflicted, Jesus is stating that the Kingdom is being offered to them preferentially, and that, especially for them, a Gospel of fraternity and liberation is "good news."

The message of the Beatitudes is present in all of the remaining discourses of Jesus about the privileged place of the poor in his Kingdom, and about the need to love them preferentially if we want to be his disciples. Among these discourses, the parable of the final judgment (Matt. 25:31–36) merits special attention. In it we find the de-mand of love for the poor with its diverse dimensions, all of them very significant for Christian spirituality. From the parable ("Come. You have my Father's blessing. . . . For I was hungry and you gave me food, . . . Out of my sight, you condemned. . . . I was hungry and you gave me no food . . ."), the meaning of the poor appears as a neces-sary condition for salvation and for acceptance in the Kingdom.

In effect, here Jesus makes explicit an important cri-terion by which he will distinguish the good from the bad. This criterion is the attitude taken toward the needy brother or sister (symbolized by the hungry, the thirsty, and so on). The one who, during his or her life, is open to the needs of the brothers and sisters who appear on the path of life will enter the Kingdom; those who are systematically closed to the poor will remain outside of it. Although we must not reduce the criteria of salvation to this parable—Jesus also indicated other criteria of sal-vation and condemnation: the love of God above all things, prayer, truth, fidelity in love, and so on—we are told here that the love of the poor forms part of the path to salvation and the Kingdom.

In the same parable, Jesus goes even further in his teaching about the poor, going so far as to identify with them: "What you did to one of these least of my brothers [or sisters—the hungry, the naked, the sick, etc.] you did it to me" (Matt. 25:40). The meaning of the poor that appears intuitive to Christianity has its ultimate evangelical root here: faith reveals the poor person to us as the sacrament of Christ, mysteriously identified with him. Again there emerges the biblical dialectic between universal fraternity and the specialness of the poor: Jesus is identified with every human being, near or far, rich or poor; Jesus is identified in a privileged way with the neighbor in need. Christ explained this identity in his teaching (". . . you did it to me") with more force than he explained any other identity. That is why we can speak of the religious dimension of the poor.

If commitment to the poor places us on the path of salvation, its gospel motivations place us on the path of holiness. Jesus' presence in the poor transforms our commitment into a path of Christian spirituality.

Furthermore, beginning above all with the teaching of St. Luke, the meaning of the poor for Jesus is not only significant for salvation or Christian spirituality. It is also significant for the evangelization or the mission of the Church. Jesus taught us that the authenticity and credibility of the Gospel depend on whether the community that evangelizes does or does not favor the poor in its preaching and in its works of human liberation. In other words, whatever the pastoral activity, whatever makes it authentic and credible to others is the option to first evangelize and liberate the poor. These are two inseparable dimensions in Jesus' teaching and activity.

In the synagogue in Nazareth (Luke 4:14ff.), Jesus

wanted to affirm the credibility of the message that he had begun to proclaim. For this he turned to the prophecy of Isaiah: "The spirit of the Lord is upon me; therefore he has anointed me. He has sent me to bring glad tidings to the poor"—the poor hold a special place in evangeliza-tion—"to proclaim liberty to captives, recovery of sight to the blind, and release to prisoners . . . "—the poor hold a special place in liberation.

It is true that the gospel meaning of Jesus' discourse points to a blindness, to an oppression, and to a captivity more interior and profound than literal; it points to the blindness, oppression, and captivity of sin. But this full meaning becomes credible and significant by the fact that it is also accompanied by liberation from literal human blindness, oppression, and captivity.

This is made clear when we see Jesus' attitude while announcing the Good News: Christ among the people al-ways united his call to faith and conversion with his com-mand to liberate the poorest from their human slavery, within their possibilities, and went to meet the occasion: "He proclaimed the Good News of the Kingdom, and cured the people of every disease and illness" (Matt. 4:23).

The same teaching, even more explicit, is found in Luke 7:18, where the disciples of the Baptist want to know if Jesus is the true Messiah or if they should expect another. John sends them to ask Christ himself. He does not answer them directly, yes or no. Better, he has them see the meaning of his actions and preaching. What is at stake is the authenticity and credibility of Jesus' gospel. "At that time he was curing many of their diseases, afflic-tions, and evil spirits; he also restored sight to many who were blind. Jesus gave this response: 'Go and report to

John what you have seen and heard. The blind recover their sight, cripples walk, lepers are cured, the deaf hear, the dead are raised, and the poor have the good news preached to them'" (Luke 7:21–22). For Jesus, that the afflicted were liberated from their slavery and that the poor received the Good News were the guarantees of the credibility of his mission.

This passage is extremely interesting taken within the context of the entire Gospel and in view of the present mission of the Church. It show us that evangelization and liberation of the poor must go hand in hand. It alerts us to the true nature of liberating evangelization.

The liberation that Jesus offered the afflicted went beyond bodily cures, as liberating as these were. Jesus socially promoted, integrated, and de-marginalized the needy. The cures of the possessed, the lepers, and the blind are typical: these were the types of people that Jesus favored in his cures, as the four evangelists testify. These are the kinds of miracles and cures that are narrated the most often.

The possessed, the blind, and the lepers were the pariahs or outcasts of that society. The lepers and possessed were considered nonhuman, despised and avoided at all costs. The blind—according to Jewish and Eastern tradition—were suspected of sin; blindness was also a moral evil: "Rabbi, was it his sin or that of his parents that caused him to be born blind?" they asked Jesus when he cured the man blind from birth (John 9:2). By returning health to these afflicted ones, Jesus liberated them from both a bodily misery and a social slavery.

These liberations were certainly partial and precarious. They were not sufficient to effect a complete liberation of these persons (because other forms of slavery were maintained, they could again become victims of those illnesses). They were not sufficient to effect global liberation that would reach to the causes and structures of the oppression of the poor. It was not within Christ's mission to resolve by himself all of the afflictions and social problems of his day, nor was this the primary objective of his cures and miracles.

The deeper meaning of these human liberations, temporary and limited as they were, lies in their manifestation that the Good News that Jesus proclaimed was an authentic and credible reality. Jesus worked enough liberations to keep alive the hope that the God of the promise, God the Liberator, was present there and that he had not forgotten his people—"God has visited his people" (Luke 7:16).

At the same time, Jesus proclaimed the Good News to the poor. He evangelized them. He called them to faith and to conversion, to what we today call interior liberation, from their sins, selfishness, and spiritual servitude. For Jesus this led to the fullness of the liberation of the poor; it guaranteed their liberation from social bondage, granting them their internal basis and ultimate meaning: "You should not be working for perishable food but for food that remains unto eternal life" (John 6:27).

In other words, the poor individual is not only socially oppressed or needy. He or she is also, like every human being, a sinner who needs conversion. Freeing the paralytic from his misery (Luke 5:17), Jesus guaranteed his power to free sinners, thus underscoring the principal content of his preaching and saving activity.

The example of Jesus' course of action is of capital importance in a pastoral activity that wants to be faithful to the meaning of the poor. Evangelization of the needy

and oppressed is not only their conscientization and join-
ing them in their human liberations and demonstrations,
nor is it only working for justice and the rights of the
weak. It is certainly all of this because otherwise the liberation that Christ brought would not be realized and the
proclamation of faith would lack credibility and historical
reference. But evangelization in the world of the poor is
an equally urgent call to conversion, to faith in Jesus, to
interior freedom, and to service to others. The poor must
also have faith and be faithful to what has been called the
option for the poor. As a Christian category, this option
for the poor is universal.

## The Experience of the Poor as Spirituality

To say that the experience of the poor is Christian
spirituality is the same as saying that efficacious love of
the poor person, service in solidarity with him or her, is
not a social or educational or cultural or political experience, but is rather a religious experience—the experience of Jesus.[3] It is the same as saying that the
experience of loving solidarity has an irreplaceable role
in the experience of the Christian God and in the spirituality that springs from that experience. It is in this
deeper sense that the poor evangelize us and the Church;
the poor are the vehicle for experience of and fidelity to
the Lord.[4]

The missionary experience is well known. Pastoral
teams and religious communities that make a lifestyle out
of the evangelizing service of the poor, experience receiving from the poor even more than they apparently
give. Their faith, their idea of Christian commitment, and
even their practice of spirituality are enriched in the

measure to which, for evangelical motives, the preferential option for the poor is incarnated in them, something to which they have been called by the Church.

This spiritual experience is very often diffuse, is not always conscious, and is not exempt from the danger of illusion or romanticism. But the experience in itself is solidly based upon a real fact, consistent with the logic of Christianity, that comes to light when we justify, according to the missionary vision of life, this greater experience of the contemporary Church: the poor evangelize us and the poor also evangelize the Church.

How can the experience of the poor be a source of spirituality? Due solely to the fact of their existence, the poor and oppressed challenge us. Whether they have or do not have certain values and qualities, whether they are good or bad, Christians or non-Christians, the reality of the poor questions our Christian and missionary conscience. Their reality helps us to discover the deeper dimensions of conversion.

Suddenly they pull us from our peacefulness and security to reveal to us in an often dramatic way the suffering and dehumanization of our brothers and sisters. They help us move from Christian individualism and show us that the imperatives of mercy, the struggle for justice, and the fraternal solidarity of our faith are unavoidable.

In summary, we better understand, experientially, that an essential dimension of conversion to the Gospel is conversion to service of the poor. And as long as this preferential option for the poor grows within us, we continue to see its demands to opt—to be converted to the poor—to change social position, mentality, and cultural values. Christian conversion is also a conversion of our prejudices and the sociocultural vision that keeps the Gospel

at arm's length—something found within every missionary. The experience of the culture of the poor and their
social position, marginated and unjust, calls us and involves us in an "exodus," a cultural and social "death" that
belongs to Christian conversion and of which we were
previously unaware.

It belongs to Christian spirituality and conversion to
the faith to lead us to see human realities, society, and
history with the eyes and standards of Jesus. These standards are different from worldly criteria. For Jesus, those
who are first shall be last, and those who are last shall be
first; the poor are blessed in the offering of the Kingdom
and the rich and wealthy are challenged; the wise and
learned of the world do not understand and the simple
and humble do. All of this is opposed to the prevalent
judgments and criteria in which power and wealth are at
the center of society and history, while the poor on the
periphery have no influence and are thus not a part of
history.

The experience of the poor helps us change this cultural vision and to gain the vision of the Gospel, the true
vision of reality, and the vision and criteria by which God
acts and through which his plan of liberating redemption
throughout history has been and is realized. The Christian
vision is that those on the periphery, the poor, are truly
the center of society and history, that from there begins
the Kingdom and that only in reference to them and in
service to them will those who are in the center share
in the Kingdom.

From the values of their religiosity, the Christian poor
live a form of popular Christian spirituality that enriches
the whole spirituality of the Church, and particularly enriches those who, through their communion of love with

the poor, are influenced by that spirituality. This "mysticism of the poor" must impregnate the various spiritualities that live together in the plurality of the Church.

The poor are subjects of a spirituality and not objects of the spirituality of the elite who opt for them. As subjects of a spiritual modality, the poor communicate spirituality at the same time they receive the spirituality of the missionary Church among them.

In effect, the popular cultures and the corresponding religion, belonging to the world of the poor, have preserved gospel attitudes and aspirations that are not commonplace in other groups, areas, or social classes. This is not the place to analyze the reason for this preservation of gospel values in the popular world, which is without a doubt linked to the fact that materialism, secularism, and rationalizations have not penetrated their culture. The fact remains that the experience of the poor is also an experience of gospel values. Yet this experience must not be idealized, because it is also marked by the ambiguity and sin of the human condition. Religious and human values are very often difficult to separate.

The poor give back to us a sense of celebration, of religious symbols, of the feast as complementary to work; they give back to us the meaning of God without complications, in the form of solidarity, hospitality, and attention to the weak who are ignored in other groups. All of this and more has a deep affinity with the Gospel, and is an experience that enriches, evangelizes, and purifies the spirituality of the entire Church.

Objectively, the experience of the poor helps us to understand and experience God, whom Jesus Christ reveals to us. We know that one of the temptations of Christian spirituality (and many other spiritualities) is that of deforming the idea of God, of making God conform to a particular culture, ideology, or teaching, or even making him conform to the God of natural religion or rational logic.

But the biblical God is different. He is a surprising and unmanipulable God, the experience of whom challenges our confused categories. He is a God whom we cannot begin to know if he does not reveal himself to us. That revelation is called Jesus of Nazareth and this Jesus is revealed to us (among other ways and special places) in the face of the poor.

The poor evangelize us because contact with their experience reminds us of a dimension of the God of Jesus that we might otherwise easily forget: that God has been inextricably linked to the human condition, to suffering, to poverty, to the forsaken, and to death by violence. Our God is a crucified God and this condition is what makes him a scandal to the "wise," while at the same time a liberating experience for the forsaken and crucified of this world. The poor evangelize us because in their face we discover the mystery of God as a God who is always greater than our ideas and conformity, a God who carries his mercy and solidarity with the human condition to the extreme.

All of this leads us to affirm that the poor are one of the privileged sacraments of the experience of Jesus among us. Jesus wants to reveal himself in a particular way in the poor and needy brother or sister, and to make service to and solidarity with that person a spiritual experience.

Out of faith and due to commitment to the poor through Jesus and his Gospel, the missionary is able to make his or her option for, and involvement among, the poor an experience of God and as such to be evangelized by this experience. Matthew's words in the parable of the final judgment, "What you did to one of the least of my brothers, you did to me," becomes a concrete missionary experience and an element of spirituality when the option for the poor becomes an encounter with the Christ of faith. In this way the Christian experience of commitment to one's neighbor, particularly the poor, begins to form part of the very experience of God, and becomes sanctifying—it evangelizes us.

The poor evangelize us because service of them widens our experience of God, makes us more contemplative, and also makes our contemplation and prayer more concrete and incarnate through uniting the experience of Jesus with the experience of the poor. Involvement among the poor, even with its limits and shortcomings (one never is able to live like them or become one of them), opens a concrete way to practice detachment and voluntary poverty. The option for the poor demands a sharing in some way of their place, their instability, their lacks, and their simplicity of life. The virtue of poverty must always have a material aspect—that is, it must be recognized as such by everyday people. The condition of the poor and suffering of our society inspires and points out the concrete options that we must make in our lifestyle in order to follow the vocation to evangelical poverty, to witness to the hope that this must offer, and to be recognized as such by others. This is the reason for the importance of gospel poverty, which the Christian spiritual tradition has always united with the efficacious love of the poor.

Evangelical poverty as freedom from and renunciation of the goods of the world has always had two basic justifications within Christian spirituality: love of identification with Jesus "who being rich made himself poor for our sake," and love of solidarity with the poor. Poverty also has its evangelical roots in the Beatitude of the poor in spirit proclaimed by Matthew (Matt. 5:3). In this Beatitude, "poverty in spirit" is a humble and total confidence in God; it is to expect everything from him and to place our lives in his hands. This attitude necessarily leads to material poverty and detachment from that which is not God. Thus, surprisingly enough, the evangelical virtue of poverty is above all grounded in our attitude toward God rather than toward things and goods.

## REFERENCES

1. Yves Congar, *El Servicio y la Pobreza en la Iglesia* (Barcelona: Estela, 1964); "A Preferential Option for the Poor," *Puebla Documents,* English edition (Washington, D.C.: Secretariat for Latin America, National Conference of Catholic Bishops, 1979), nn. 1134–65; Segundo Galilea, *El Sentido del Pobre* (Bogotá: Indoamerican Press, 1978); A. Paoli, *Diálogo de la Liberación* (Buenos Aires: Lohle, 1970), *La Perspectiva Política de San Lucas* (Siglo XXI).
2. Segundo Galilea, *El Sentido de Pobre.*
3. Gustavo Gutiérrez, *Revelación y Anuncio de Dios en la Historia* (Lima: CEP, 1976), *Teología desde el Reverso de la Historia* (Lima: CEP, 1977).
4. *Puebla Documents,* nn. 1147.

# 7. The Way of the Cross

## The Experience of the Cross as Spirituality

What we have come to call the cross or crosses in the language of spirituality (terms belonging to Christian cultures), is simply the sufferings and contradictions of life. The cross is a fact of the human condition; neither Jesus nor medieval mysticism invented it.[1]

In themselves, such crosses have no inherent value; they are a negative human experience that no one is called to seek. But on the other hand they are an inescapable fact, before which we as human beings must assume an attitude and to which we must give meaning.

In Christianity these crosses find their meaning, not because Christianity teaches us how to eliminate a cross or make a value out of a cross, but because, due to Christ who assumed our human condition including suffering and the cross, the experience of the cross can now be sanctifying and even liberating for us and finds its place in the coming of the Kingdom.

Because of Christ, the fact of the cross can be accepted as a dimension of spirituality. This is how we understand Jesus' call to "take up the cross," "to carry one's cross daily," "to lose one's life," or "to die like the grain of wheat" (Matt. 11:12; 16:21–24; 17:15; John 12:24–26).

Only by following Christ are we caused by the cross to grow in the life according to the Spirit. The previous reflections have shown us that there is not a separate "spirituality of the cross," just as there is not a separate spirituality of poverty or of obedience or self-denial, but rather one basic spirituality of discipleship. That is the fundamental value of Christian spirituality. It is following Jesus through the Spirit who leads us to poverty, self-denial, or the cross. The cross is not sought for itself; it is found as a spiritual value the more we follow Jesus.

The cross as a dimension of spirituality has three aspects. First, the cross forms part of the human condition. We are limited and vulnerable; illness, frustration, suffering, and death are integral parts of our life. To live this experience of life in the way of Christ—who taught us to live human limitations as children of God—is already spirituality. Through faith we know that the dynamic of the cross and death within us forms part of the paschal dynamic of Christian life, and by clothing ourselves in the suffering and yet risen Jesus, life according to the Spirit is communicated to us. The Christian experience of the cross is a paschal experience.

Second, the Christian cross is the price and path of conversion. Because we are immersed in egoism and the tendency toward sin, the path of conversion to following Jesus through the Spirit is a path of overcoming, of the "death of the old man" (Rom. 6), of renouncing life "according to the flesh" (Matt. 18:8; Luke 14:33). There is no Christian conversion or any human improvement and renewal without that form of the cross that is the renunciation of ourselves. This is what Christ means by his call to follow him "carrying our cross daily."

Third, the cross as suffering and contradiction, as persecution and even death, is a result of faithful commitment to Jesus and his Gospel of the Kingdom. This is the richest and most important dimension of the cross in Christian spirituality because it is the clearest way that Christ experienced the cross. The great proof of love and discipleship is to be identified with Jesus, who was persecuted and martyred on account of the Kingdom.

That is why persecution and martyrdom are a Beatitude (Matt. 5:10–12; Luke 6:22–23). In a special way, the cross of the witness to the faith in and the justice of the Kingdom, imitates Christ and causes us to be reborn. In one way, this Beatitude summarizes the experience of the cross as a Christian value.

The persecution that the Beatitudes proclaim includes every form of contradiction to the Kingdom—"rejected, slandered, every sort of evil spoken against you"—of which martyrdom is the highest form. The spiritual experience of the cross has thus been constant in the life of the Church, and is even now being undergone by those currently persecuted and martyred in the cause of the justice of the Kingdom.

## Fidelity to the Spirit in Times of Conflict

Conflict is one of the most common guides in which the cross presents itself in the human condition.[2] Individuals, families, human communities, society, and above all the Church have experienced and continue to experience situations of conflict. Thus conflict is a fact, often unavoidable and often linked to and strengthened by selfishness and sin, but many times also the simple consequence of the fact that each of us is unique, limited, and at times incompatible.

In any case, conflict of any kind is one form of the cross and suffering, and as such must be integrated within spirituality. Jesus experienced conflict in a very harsh way during his public ministry: conflicts with religious leaders, with those in public power, misunderstanding on the part of the people and the disciples, his passion and cross, were the tragic and inevitable result of the conflictive nature of Jesus' life. He who did not seek conflict, who brought a message of mercy and fraternity, knew one of the most dramatic experiences of conflict in human history because of the rejection and reaction of sinners.

But we have said that conflict is not always attributable to moral evil. It is a normal fact of life that must be embraced by spirituality. Paradoxically, the first conflict that appeared in Jesus' life—the conflict between Jesus and his mother (Luke 2:41–51)—was this type of conflict. The episode of Jesus lost in the temple was conflictive event. Jesus disappeared, his worried parents searched for him, and once they found him they did not understand Jesus' attitude. The interesting thing about this conflict is that both parties were correct; there were no "good guys" and "bad guys." It was a misunderstanding stemming from love and without negative consequences; no breakdown of their relationship resulted.

Jesus lost and found in the temple is the paradigm of all healthy, familiar, and inevitable conflicts because it took place in the encounter of two fidelities. It is the paradigm of conflicts within the Church. Not all, or even many, of the conflicts within the Church, both past and present, have been or are the products of pride, infidelity, stupidity, or blindness. Many times the parties in conflict have their reasons and are faithful to the Spirit. But the conflict arises anyway because of the incompatibility of those fidelities, because of misunderstanding, or because of the simple, blameless limitation of the individuals involved.

The Americas are passing through a stage of history that is particularly conflictive. It is common to refer to social, cultural, and economic conflicts. These conflicts are clearly reflected in the Church. One significant component of the Christian experience is its conflicts, very often generated by its mission and by its defense of justice, generated by the demands of Christian prophecy. All of these experiences are neither extraordinary nor heroic; they were foreseen and widely proclaimed by Jesus himself (Matt. 24; Mark 13; Luke 17; 19).

Our challenge is to integrate, in the light of the Gospel and the spiritual tradition of the Church, fidelity and conflict into one experience of identification with Jesus through the Spirit. This does not mean to create a spirituality of conflict or to overvalue conflict in some way. Again, conflict and the cross are never values in themselves; and it would be very improper to speak of a spirituality of conflict. If, however, we can speak of a Christian spirituality "within conflict," it must remain true that the one authentic spirituality in Christianity is the one that springs from following Jesus under the guidance of the Church. It is not the conflict that sanctifies but rather the identification with Jesus, who was subject to conflict and persecution. This following of Christ not only comes to be one of the causes of conflict between his disciples but it is also the model of how to live with conflicts in a human and gospel way—in a word, how to live the experience of conflict as spirituality. The following reflections may help us understand this further.

### How to Live with Conflict

The one fundamental value of Christian spirituality is love according to Christ's law, to love God and to love one's brothers and sisters indiscriminately because every human being is a sacrament of the absolute God. All the other values, virtues, or options of spirituality matter only to the extent that they express or are capable of generating love. That is why St. Paul was able to write that without charity, apparently generous acts such as faith, prophecy, or commitment to the cause of the poor are worth nothing in regard to the imitation of Christ (1 Cor. 13:1ff.).

It must be affirmed, therefore, that the conflicts of Christian life and mission, even for just causes, lose their evangelical value if they are met without love. Experience teaches us that the conflicts of Christian life are justified by a twofold love. Either the cause of God and his Kingdom is what is at stake or it is the cause of the individual, both of which are inseparable and intertwined. The conflicts that are lived today by Christians are the result of living Christian love within a historical and social context, just as the conflicts in the life of Jesus stemmed from the collision between the demands of his love and an unjust and sinful reality. Like the master, the disciple of Jesus does not bring on conflict for its own sake; rather, conflict arises and is revealed as a result of the disciple's giving witness to the demands of love. Furthermore, by touching upon conflict and embracing it, the disciple brings human and evangelical values to bear upon it so as to overcome and solve conflict.

The radical solution of human conflicts is contained in the dynamic of Christian love, a universal love and, at the same time, a love that makes choices. Surprisingly, the universality of love and the reality of its options is, on the one hand, one of the conditions for overcoming conflicts, and, on the other, often the historical cause of conflicts in the Christian life.

Indiscriminate and universal love as well as the options themselves of the incarnation of love in society are sources of conflict. Jesus' own practice also demonstrates this. The universality of love in a divided society—and in a Church that is shaken in the same way although in other terms—is in the long run conflictive. It is placed unjustly between two flames and so it is a source of misunderstanding or wrong interpretation on all sides. When sectarianism becomes the sociocultural way of life (even sometimes within Christian communities), remaining universal becomes highly painful and conflictive.

But the same thing could be said about the option of Christian love and so about its commitments. The subject is all too well known, and the conflicts that are created by the options of Christian charity do not need any further elaboration. The preferential option for the poor and oppressed, the struggle for justice and for the rights and dignity of each human being, have been thoroughly discussed. One only needs to remember that these are practices of Christian love, of Christian mysticism, and not only social or pastoral activism. These options are essential to spirituality. To make these choices is to follow Jesus in today's history, with all of the inevitable conflicts for the life of his disciples.

But we also said, that, paradoxically, Christian love as universality and as fundamental options is also the only trusted key to evangelical resolution of conflicts. To overcome conflicts there must be great love—this much is true. But even further, expressions of love are needed to overcome conflict and these expression are, precisely, its universality and the option for the poor and for justice. Out of the universality of love we know that the final point of conflict is its reconciliation, and that this attitude of love, although it may not be possible to achieve in fact, must be present in all options and struggles. In the same way, without justice for the poor and oppressed there is no real solution of conflicts, even within the Church. The dynamic of Christian love as the healing of conflicts supposes a synthesis between universality and options, between justice and reconciliation. It supposes a struggle for the poor with a reconciled heart. We know all too well that this synthesis is not easy; it is itself an expression of gospel spirituality within the conflict.

There are purely exterior human conflicts (persecutions, accusations, or contradictions that come solely from outside). Every human conflict is such because there is always an interior dimension that is perceived as a crisis of the spirit. Conflict and crisis go hand in hand. Therefore, conflict has to do with spirituality and can be integrated with spirituality.

Crisis is the result of a more or less conscious self-questioning. Our way of living certain values and the very synthesis that we have made of the Christian and missionary life are brought into question. Crisis is a time of insecurity that calls for a new synthesis of values and a new gospel living of those same values. Conflict creates crisis because it insists upon a rethinking, a deepening, and it pulls us from our apparent stability and conformity.

In this sense, conflict and crisis are a call to a gradual conversion. They are a call to deepen the globality of Christian commitment and to grow in all of the values that conflict has put into crisis. There is no Christian— or human—maturity and there is no development of an adult spirituality without passage through the crises of conflict. Conflict leads to maturity and demands maturity to be embraced and overcome. The fact that at times conflicts destroy persons or weaken faith and spirituality or lead to the dismissal of Christian options betrays the Christian notion of conflict and crisis. These cases reveal immaturity or lack of a true spirituality within conflict. In the Gospel, conflict and crisis are the way toward spiritual maturity.

We could say, then, that God is also revealed within conflict. In its own disconcerting and mysterious way, conflict is the Lord's call, a personal or collective grace to enable us to follow the persecuted and slandered Jesus with a firmer option and out of motives greatly purified by the Gospel. As God's call, conflict is disconcerting and must remain disconcerting. Given the human condition and given historical reality, where egoism, lies, and injustice are ever-latent, crisis and conflict are often the historical grace that God offers us so that we can mature in freedom, truth, and justice.

But there are crises and conflicts that are very prolonged, no matter what their external cause may be. There are very difficult tensions, tensions within the Church, the products not only of divisions but also of legitimate pluralism. There are social tensions due to the struggle for justice or to the diverse options that this leads to. There are tensions and disagreements within the Christian consciousness, generally as a result of options that are difficult to make when we are faced with ambiguous alternatives, perplexities, and conflicts of values in very complex situations. In these cases and in others, we need enough maturity to live within these situations of tension and conflict, both prolonged and structural, without breaking, without becoming radicalized, without backing down, and without rejecting fundamental values. To maintain this maturity and to grow in it is also part of spirituality in situations of conflict, of crisis, and of tension.

This, maturity—both human and evangelical—should make us understand that conflict is not of value in itself and that we should not promote conflict. Conflict will come. Christian spirituality does not mean not having conflicts or making them disappear as soon as they arise. Spirituality is how we respond to crises and conflicts, how and with what spirit we embrace them, what meaning we give them, and what we do with them. And as we have repeatedly mentioned, reference to the practice of Jesus is indispensable. His attitude toward the crisis, tension, and conflict that in fact framed his life is what forms the basis for any valid Christian attitude and spirituality.

Christian spirituality is a spirituality of synthesis—synthesis of options, attitudes, and values that are seemingly difficult to integrate, such as prayer action, love struggle, demands understanding, mercy justice, prudence risk, and so on. To embrace conflict with a spirit of maturity and as a call to growth also requires a synthesis of values and attitudes—as we have already pointed out. If we embrace conflict in this spirit, there can be no rupture or backing down or struggle without love and reconciliation, no pacifying love without respecting the rights of the poor and human dignity.

## Gospel Attitudes in the Face of Conflict

Conflict may be accepted but it is not fabricated. It is accepted evangelically but is not sought as a value in itself, whether for reasons of prestige or because it may be fashionable. There can be subtle pride in being persecuted by the powers of this world or in the cause of the poor; there is such a thing as the vanity of the prophet. The truth is that it is God who creates prophets, always in spite of themselves. Having a prophet or persecution complex, seeking that situation, makes Christian spirituality suspect in the face of conflict. Conflict is lived in a Christian way by forgetting about it, by not looking at it. There is always the risk that crisis and conflict may give rise to a form of narcissism or some other form of pharisaism.

Along this same line, we must recognize that conflict in our life is not only the consequence of our Christian witness but also of our errors and even sins. In Jesus' life, persecution and conflict were absolutely unjust because Christ was absolutely just. In our case, conflict in our life is not always totally unjust because we are not always just. We commit errors, we are unjust, and we lack education; often we lack love in the defense of the cause of the Kingdom. Therefore, conflicts in Christian life are also a path of purification, of learning. This should keep us humble at those times when we experience the Beatitude of persecution.

Although we are always in search of a more evangelical attitude on the path of our crises and conflicts, the spirituality that accompanies this must always be nourished by hope. To remain faithful and whole amid conflicts and persecutions is a proof of hope—of our belief that evil and injustice do not have the final word in history, that reality is not only what is seen and experienced (struggle, oppression, resistance to the Kingdom, the apparent failure of good) but is also what Christ has revealed, his promises of the Kingdom that we do not immediately experience (see, for instance; Heb. 11:1ff., on faith and hope proved and nurtured in conflict and contradition—"Moses persevered [despite everything] as if he were looking upon the invisible God").

To weather conflicts is hope in the sense that by understanding our contradiction from the standpoint of Jesus' experience, we know that there is nothing irredeemable, nothing fatal, and nothing that is irreversible. The role of spirituality in tribulation and failure is to enable us to begin again, faithfully, by virtue of hope in the one who "makes all things new." Finally, this hope leads to interior freedom before every kind of power and seduction, wealth or career (even within the Church) that we need in order to not give in to conflict, to be faithful, and to not make a pact between the spirit of the world and the demands of the gospel. Only those who have nothing to lose (prestige, career, security) are capable of remaining faithful—even to the conflict of the cross—and thereby maintaining the spirituality of hope.

Spirituality in times of conflict is one thing, and being conflictive is another. The latter has to do with culpable conflict, which does not come from the collision between our faithfulness to the Kingdom and conscious or unconscious resistance to it. The spiritual aspect of conflict invites us to be nonconflictive—that is, to overcome the spirit of sectarianism or the incapacity for communion and dialogue with those who do not share our way of fidelity. The spirit of sectarianism that must be overcome in this case is one that sees those who suffer conflict as necessarily being good and all others as being bad, leading to a confusion between the prophets whose vision comes from God and those who burn their bridges with their community. The prophet with a spirituality is not systematically aggressive and does not break with his or her ecclesial institution or with those who form it.

One must avoid the temptation to bring to the Church those categories and methods that are utilized by social and ideological struggles and political conflicts. Within the Christian community, the supreme value of fraternity—communion and sharing—does not exclude tensions, crises, and arguments but rather gives rise to a spirituality in which these are dealt with according to gospel attitudes.

Active and historical patience is another important attitude regarding conflict. Not everything can be resolved or realized immediately. One must believe in God's own time, that there is an hour when he always turns up. We must value the time factor and discern when time will contribute to the resolution of a conflict or when it is better to intervene to diminish it.

Simple acceptance of the fact that reality—and the Church as part of it—has a normal conflictive dimension is already a gospel attitude. Furthermore, we must accept that we are the protagonists in normal conflict, that we are the ones discussed, rejected, or under suspicion. Like Jesus, we cannot be understood and accepted by every type of person (given the conflict between types), despite our good will. We must accept not having everyone's trust. A certain solitude is part of any prophet's life, and we must accept it without being surprised or feeling victimized.

Very often conflicts arise when, on account of fidelity to the Gospel and to the Church, we take positions that at the time are considered suspicious within the community or that are not favored by prevailing public opinion or by those sectors whose interests are threatened by any position of social prophecy. In that case, we share in some way in Christian prophecy (which basically means a desire to be faithful to the truth). These situations create a new conflict for the believer between fidelity to the choice made and fidelity to the body of the Church. Resolution of these situations requires a spirituality that, in the long run, can be discerned, just as the true prophet can be discerned from the false.

To be faithful in conflict implies a synthesis of attitudes whose achievement is already guaranteed by fidelity itself, an attitude of not breaking either with the ecclesial community or with dialogue. (This is a profound and fundamental attitude and not something purely psychological, as if the relationship were easy and that it were easy to be comfortable with being in agreement or sympathy.) This is an attitude of knowing how to wait, of going more slowly when this facilitates communion; it is an attitude of being willing to obey, to change or retract a position without ceasing to work for and seek that which is the Christian ideal in the situation. This requires valuing suffering and the cross of conflicts as purifying paths of maturity and life. It requires not only learning to suffer for the Church but above all because of it, which is the greatest proof of faithful love.

There is no mature Christian spirituality without a sense of humor. And this applies even more urgently to spirituality in times of conflict and crisis. A sense of humor becomes subtle proof that gospel attitudes are present. Bitterness, dramatics, demagoguery in the use of conflict are opposed to the Christian sense of humor. On the contrary, the Christian attitude is undramatic serenity, holding on to optimism and joy (profound joy and not necessarily external-psychological happiness), and this attitude marks the degree of humor that normally accompanies mature love. There is no Christian love without humor.

The Christian sense of humor is not to take oneself or the protagonists of conflict very seriously. It is to know how to laugh at oneself, to take distance from conflict and to see it in an objective and always relative perspective. The Christian sense of humor insures the good will of intentions, the spirit of tolerance and reconciliation, and finally, the ability to relativize and see conflicts in their proper proportion, from a place of faith and not of emotion. Amid tensions and conflicts, a healthy sense of humor, a joke, a smile are all a form of fraternal communion.

Finally, this spiritual maturity that is called a sense of humor implies that we have faith in values that transcend the individual situations, decisions, and prestige involved in a conflict. Christians know that human beings are of more value than a conflict, and this conviction only becomes real if we support the humanization of struggle and conflict not only with justice, but also with good nature and a sense of humor.

## REFERENCES

1. Leonardo Boff, *Pasión de Cristo, pasión del mundo* (Bogotá: Indoamerican Press, 1978); Jürgen Moltmann, *The Crucified God* (New York: Harper & Row, 1974); Segundo Galilea, *Espiritualidad de la Evangelización* (Bogotá: CLAR, 1980).
2. José Marins, *Iglesia y Conflicto Social en América Latina* (Bogotá: Paulinas, 1975); CLAR, *Fidelidad y Conflicto en la Vida Religiosa* (Bogotá: CLAR, 1981).

# 8. Spirituality and Mission

## In Search of a Missionary Spirituality

In this chapter we want to touch upon a spirituality of mission; we will not develop here a theology of mission or discuss in depth the conditions for missionary pastoral activity. Although the theme of a spirituality of mission has already been treated implicitly throughout the whole of this book, we wish to present a special chapter dedicated to the privileged place that mission has in Christian life and in the Church.[1]

Mission is an exalted form of following Jesus. To follow Jesus is to collaborate with him in the liberating salvation of the world, which is an extension of the Kingdom of God. Following and mission appear side by side in the gospel. Jesus called the Twelve to follow him and to proclaim the Kingdom of God: "Peter, do you love me? . . . Then feed my sheep" (Mark 1:16ff.; 3:23ff.; John 21:15ff.).

Because mission is following , Christ is the only model for mission. To follow the missionary Jesus, sent by the Father, is to "missionize" like him, with his criteria, attitudes, options, and with the same spirituality as him. Every teaching about the spirituality of mission must necessarily refer to the way and the spirit with which Christ realized his mission.

Speaking of the spirit of mission, we must remember that the idea of mission has different degrees and depths. In one sense, there is only one idea of mission: the Church and its Christians are always and everywhere on mission, although in different ways depending on the situation and challenges of faith. In this sense, the Church is involved in the same mission whether in Spain or in Bangladesh. In a second sense, mission tends to be radicalized by its own dynamic; that is, it goes beyond itself and its boundaries to reach the most neglected and the least evangelized. This dynamic comes from the very fact of following Christ: "Go and make disciples of all nations" (Matt. 28:18).

In this way, the dynamic of mission is the dynamic of exodus—cultural, geographic, and religious. Mission is to leave one's own geographic or cultural Christian world in order to enter the world of even the poorest and the most un-Christian. The nonbeliever, the fallen-away Christian, the poor, and the oppressed are always the subject of missionary love, and the more mission leaves its own world in search of them, the more it is radicalized and the closer it approaches the model and desire of Christ.

It is in this most radical sense that missionary practice achieves its proper depth, in a pure state. It is there that the spiritual conditions for all mission are best perceived. Mission does not have its own special spirituality; its spirituality is always Christian spirituality and, as such, there can be no spirituality of mission without Christian identity, without conversion, without the experience of God, without fraternal love, without love of the poor and abandoned, without poverty, and without acceptance of persecution and the cross. But because mission is based on a state of exodus, which is a particular form of death to self and of following Jesus, it can be said rightly that mission demands a particular spirituality.

The spirit of the missionary is part of the content of

his or her message and efficacy. The same is not true of other human activities in which professional competence can be separated from the lifestyle of the individual. The missionary option is not an accidental or imposed option; existentially, it forms part of the life plan of the person. The missionary exodus radically colors the life of a Christian. The missionary's lifestyle is the sign of the credibility of the Gospel that is shared with others and thus must be absolutely consistent with that Gospel. What might be dispensable when one dwells among believers becomes a decisive matter when one deals with those outside of the Church. By lifestyle and spirituality, the missionary incarnates the transcendent, mysterious, and disconcerting aspects of mission within a human reality and culture.

## Conditions of a Missionary Spirituality

### *Contemplation*

First of all, the missionary must be a contemplative, capable of transmitting not only ideas, discourses, and analyses but above all his or her personal experience of Jesus Christ and the values of his Kingdom. Within the heart of the distant masses, the contemplative witness of a Christian is frequently the only vehicle by which the light of the Gospel is communicated. The more we enter into the periphery of Christianity, the "strange land," the more we must remain one with the contemplative sources of the Church. Many generous missionaries are waylaid or lose their Christian identity by forgetting this.

Someone has defined the missionary as "the one who acts as if he saw the invisible God." The missionary is the one who is able to carry on beyond any difficulty, any frustration, or any deception because he or she has the strength to act as though seeing God out of a personal Christian experience. This is the source of missionary hope. For this reason, when we speak of the spirit of mission, we cannot avoid the question of the faith experience of the missionary. Only faith and contemplation put us face-to-face with the invisible God.

The missionary is the one who gives himself or herself to the building up of a kingdom that goes beyond who the individual is or what he or she does. Contemplation is the mode of action that results from faith experience, and the contemplative mode of action is marked by hope. It is marked by serenity in the face of the colossal missionary task before us. In the perspective of faith, mission is doing what God wants, when God wants it, and not what we think should be done. The first attitude is the source of hope; the latter is the source of discouragement and frustration.

Mission is a call, a vocation, by which God sends us out to others (Gal. 1:15). The missionary call is a projection toward others, a dynamic always to go beyond the limits. This dynamic is exhausted if it is not continually nurtured by the contemplative experience. The missionary call is not an obligation but the dynamic result of an encounter with the living Christ.

There is a biblical ideal of the contemplative missionary. The prophets are the model. From Moses down through Elijah, the prophets of the Exile, and John the Baptist to Jesus Christ himself, the biblical prophet is one sent by God to call people to follow the one, only, and unchanging God and to denounce all idolatry. At the same time the prophet is a disciple whose heart God has purified and to whom he has been revealed in an often dramatic religious experience.

In biblical symbolism, the prophet is alternately sent to the city as an evangelizer and then led to the desert to deepen his or her experience of God. Moses, Elijah and the other prophets, John the Baptist, and Jesus himself prepared their mission in the desert and often returned there. The desert, more than a place, is a biblical symbol. On the one hand it is the place of solitude and poverty where the heart is purified, idols are toppled, and the real and exclusive encounter with God is realized. It is the place of Christian contemplation. On the other hand, the desert is the symbol of the sterility and hardness of the human heart to which the prophet is sent. The Baptist preached in the desert; the prophet evangelizes a sinful society.

The biblical prophets are models of the Christian missionary. What appear to be alternations in the life of the missionary (mission in the city and the experience of God in the desert) symbolize what must be simultaneously realized as two inseparable dimensions of the Christian life. Every missionary is called to make this synthesis, to unite the courage of prophetic commitment with the contemplative experience of God.

## Poverty

Mission demands poverty both as a condition and as a way of life—not just any poverty (we know that gospel poverty can be expressed in many ways) but missionary poverty. Missionary poverty goes beyond the ordinary demands of poverty in evangelization characterized by involvement among the poor, an austere lifestyle, and the option of solidarity for the cause of the oppressed. There is the further impoverishment of the missionary inherent in the exodus to a "strange land." This impoverishment, in both attitude and lifestyle, is demanded by the ecclesial as well as cultural exodus.

The ecclesial exodus, in mission, is to leave one's own church (with its Christian surroundings) to go and strengthen another, weaker church, or to plant it as a sign of the Kingdom where it does not yet exist. In any event, there is no missionary exodus without abandoning the ways of an established church or conventional evangelization in order to place oneself at the service of another model of Church. The missionary must die, must be impoverished, to everything that can prevent seeing, feeling, and acting in service to another Christian reality.

The cultural exodus is to abandon one's own culture, with its Christian symbolism and interpretation, in order to be immersed in another culture. This does not mean simply adapting to the new (as much as possible) but rather bringing about its evangelization through a Christian reinterpretation of that culture. Without the mutually enriching symbiosis between faith and culture, the Gospel cannot enter into the human medium. This is the reason for the demand for cultural impoverishment on the part of the missionary, not in the sense of totally casting off the values of the culture of origin, but in the sense of being freed from that culture's conditioning which prevents the perception of the Spirit and the proper paths of the Gospel in the culture of the "strange land" that the missionary has come to serve.

Missionary poverty, like every other form of gospel poverty, is a risk in hope. It is a leap into the abyss, supported by the faith of the Church. The missionary exodus is frightening, just as it was for the missionary-prophets of the God of Israel, sent by their Lord to lands of exile to keep alive faith in the promise. Poverty in mission is to accept crises of insecurity and of the many forms of rebirth without losing one's Christian identity. Missionary impoverishment requires a great deal of maturity; it is not for adolescent Christians or for those in search of escape or publicity stunts.

### Self-confidence

Mission requires self-confidence. Said another way, the missionary must believe and trust in the Spirit that animates the Church and in the often obscure and mysterious efficacy of evangelization and the means appropriate to the missionary effort. "I chose you to go forth and bear fruit, and that your fruit may endure" (John 15:16).

The tragedy is that many do not believe in evangelization's own and irreducible efficacy, especially when faced with others. This lack of confidence substitutes the easier and more consoling work with believers alone or with material projects in place of the missionary dynamic. Sometimes what is substituted is the apparently more visible and immediate efficacy of human rationality or politics. The current situation of missionary despair is owed in large part to these temptations. When mission is separated from Jesus' perspective of redemption and his Kingdom, it can be bogged down by any valid human enterprise or ideal and by their means and ends. Mission, which necessarily includes human criteria of efficacy, always transcends these criteria because of its radical objective of conversion to Jesus and to fraternal love, overcoming sin, and the experience of God the Father. These radical objectives and liberations imply the activity of God's gift and grace upon his people and the sharing in Jesus' prayer and sacrifice.

As a person who has faith in the dynamic of mission and the strength of its message, the missionary believes in the mysteriously liberating efficacy of the daily cross as well as that of his or her presence and personal surrender among the people or amid disbelief. The missionary believes in the value of holiness and surrender in and of themselves. He or she believes in the qualitative strength of mission and Christian presence. Although those who cross the boundaries of their churches to go among others may be in the minority, their ecclesial significance is incalculable; they are the small remnant that represents the entire Church and that acts in its name, signifying the coming of the Kingdom of God among others.

This trust in mission and in the coming of the Kingdom "against all hope" gives rise to real patience and Christian meekness in the face of the contradictions and failures of mission. The ultimate root of this attitude, which we identify with the "meek and humble of heart" missionary Christ, is the poverty of spirit according to the Beatitudes. Radical poverty of spirit not only consciously and actively places our mission in God's hands but also leads us to follow the attitudes in mission of Christ, who, because he was poor and dependent upon the Father and poor among his brothers and sisters, "did not crush the bruised reed or quench the smoldering wick" nor was "his voice heard in the streets" (Matt. 12:19–20).

Confidence in the work of Christ's spirit in mission is made known through respect for every person, through nonimposition, through recognition of truth and goodness where they are encountered, through humility, and through disinterest in self. This gospel style in mission forms part of the Christian witness that makes it credible and acceptable, through patience and the cross.

### Itinerancy

Missionary spirituality calls for a spirit of itinerancy and acceptance of the provisional. By its very nature, mission is exodus, dynamic and mobile. When its essential objective has been assured, it does not become entrenched in an established community or in work with those already converted but always begins a new exodus. It always goes beyond, seeking out those who are most alienated, most poor, and most in need of the Gospel.

This means that while respecting individual pastoral situations and personal vocations, the missionary must maintain a spiritual attitude consistent with this demand, one of promoting local ministries and leadership so he or she can be replaced as soon as possible. Accordingly, a noncareer attitude, necessary for the profound freedom of every evangelizer, is essential to the missionary in order to maintain acceptance of a provisional life and to respond to the call to go beyond, when this call is felt.

The missionary experiences tension between his or her involvement and commitment with a local community and the readiness to move on and disengage when the time comes. The synthesis of both attitudes, realized in all their seriousness and without sacrificing one for the other, requires a particular spirituality, which is the gift of the missionary vocation. This spirituality of itinerancy, like any other Christian spirituality, has as its model and only reference following Jesus in his condition as an itinerant evangelizer and as a uniting apostle among the Jewish people of his time.

For this attitude of exodus and itinerancy to enrich the missionary and the community, it must have its roots in the Christian experience of the individual missionary; and he or she must also carry the richness of his or her church of origin. Involvement in another church and culture must never occur at the price of emptying the missionary of the message and particular treasure that the Church is offering to catholicity at this time in history.

## REFERENCES

1. *Ad Gentes*, nn. 23–27; Paul VI, *Evangelii Nuntiandi*; J. Loew, *Perfil del Apostol Hoy*, 4th ed. (Estella: Verbo Divino, 1970); CLAR, *La Misión desde América Latina* (Bogotá: CLAR, 1982); Segundo Galilea, *La Responsabilidad Misionera de América Latina* (Bogotá: Paulinas, 1981).